EXECUTIVE SUMMARY

This study argues that the spread of violent extremism cannot be fully understood as an ideological or social phenomenon, but must be viewed as a process that integrates the two forces in a coevolutionary manner. The same forces that make an ideology appealing to some aggrieved group of people are not necessarily the same factors that promote its transfer through social networks of self-interested human beings.

As a result, radicalization inexorably intertwines social and ideological forces in systemic fashion. The coevolutionary nature of the social and ideological spheres presents a unique challenge and is one of the reasons that rigorous efforts to identify a radical or terrorist profile have not yielded significant return. Efforts to develop an archetype often focuses on individual traits, but it may be that profiles based on social and ideological behavior need to be considered simultaneously in developing a theory that is actionable for counterterrorism practitioners.

Key insights from the theoretical and empirical discussions that follow provide new insights into the social patterns of violent extremists over time, which are important to understanding radicalization.

The analysis of domestic terrorism data shows that, to date, there is little evidence of lone wolf jihadists. There are very few people who progress to violent action in isolation, and those that do so are often motivated by other forces such as mental health issues or other political grievances. Many radicals have a history of social contact or reaching out to develop relationships with like-minded individuals.

Social relationships follow a nonlinear pattern. They are increasingly important in the early stages of radicalization and peak when people accept a violent doctrine. Developing new relationships becomes less important once individuals come to adopt radical beliefs. The empirical analysis suggests that the search for external validation of radical ideas is most important in the early stages of an individual's radicalization and declines in importance once the barriers to entry are overcome.

There is also a nonlinear relationship observed in the data analyzed here between social ties and ideological affinity, whereby those primed for affinity through exposure to radical ideas in early schooling have as many close social ties as those with completely secular schooling. Individuals in between these two extremes averaged fewer close connections, which challenges conventional wisdom about ideological predisposition and social relationships.

The importance of self-serving extremism has not been well recognized. Individuals who recruit others gain social status for their efforts, meaning that the spread of extremism may be just as much a function of self-interest as ideological fervor. This has important implications understanding and countering violent extremism.

The growth of radical groups is a self-organizing process driven by aggregation of individual behavior, where the entry catalyst into an extremist cell most likely takes the form of someone who recruits one, two or three other participants. This self-organization produces cells that have many close-knit people, or can easily access others, meaning that such groups are well suited to facilitation and monitoring. By contrast, such cells are much less likely to have many gatekeepers or brokers who operate between cliques.

There are number of insights and implications that follow from the qualitative and quantitative analyses in this paper:

Conceptual Precision in Countering Radical Ideology

Countering radical ideology is probably perceived or defined differently across the spectrum of pertinent actors, but it is unlikely that success will come from falsifying an idea or finding the loophole that invalidates an ideology. Rather, it will require a process whereby the ineffective and corrupt nature of the radical ideas must be displayed repeatedly over time. In pursuit of this end, the way that humans rewire themselves, either socially or neurologically, to accept radical ideas being advanced may be more important than the ideas themselves.

Defusing Radicalization and the Role of Social Stages

Disrupting radicalization early may seem the easiest route to preventing people from pursuing violent ends, but the barriers to entry in the early stages of awareness and interest are rather low. The best place to disrupt radicalization is the area where the personal barriers are greatest, the acceptance stage, when individuals seek social ties to overcome normative constraints on violent action. Platforms must be developed that are capable of identifying people already working through the early stages and geared to intervene by redirecting individuals in the later stages.

Extremist Websites and the Facebook-ization of the Internet

Social media offers prospective radicals an opportunity to develop social ties and find validation through others, thus providing the critical element of social interaction at relatively low cost. Traditional push avenues of radicalization like YouTube and extremist websites help communicate ideas, but the personalization of the Internet and online relationships is an evolving arena that can make extremist propaganda interactive in very dangerous ways. Each aspect of this issue represents a newly emerging trend, meaning that not much is known about these processes.

Counterculture and Jihad

The instances that come closest to lone wolf jihadist activities represent a different troubling trend that is best described as the conjoining of jihad and counterculture activity. Many of the Americans who turn toward jihad to express their political grievances have a history of counterculture activity prior to violent activity, and the concept of "jihadi cool" makes extremism not simply a devout life choice but a socially redeeming and adventurous pathway.

Radicalization Pathways and Threat Assessment

There are different ways that individuals may progress through the stages of radicalization, with different implications for interdiction and crisis management. People who skip stages in radicalization are likely to radicalize quickly and also spend less time planning than those who do not. By contrast, individuals who progress along the prototypical radicalization process offer more time for interdiction, but may utilize the additional planning time to develop a more sophisticated attack. Further, an individual who has undergone a longer radicalization process probably has developed more extensive social ties that can be leveraged for resources or knowledge.

Socially Self-Serving Extremism

In an attempt to understand sources of violent extremism, emphasis on the underlying ideological doctrine may have masked a simple factor driving its spread: good old-fashioned social standing and self-interest. Individuals who recruit others tend to have better social standing in a group over time. Ideological doctrine is critical to understanding a radical movement, but it may play less of a role in explaining why the movement spreads and changes as it does than understanding the social benefits involved for those who actively spread the ideas and find new adherents.

Next Steps in Decoding Radicalization

There is a great deal to be done in the study of violent extremism and two areas will prove tremendously important in the development of efficient and effective policies. First, almost all studies of radicalization to date have no variance in the independent variable radicalization, meaning that they capture patterns of radicalization among a sample where everyone is a radical. The second is the importance of addressing the receptivity to violent ideology, rather than just ideology itself, to include the biological, neurobiological, and social-psychological process that occur as people come to adopt new radical views.

INTRODUCTION

Violent extremism presents one of the greatest threats to the citizenry of the United States and its allies. It does not represent an existential threat to the United States or the international system, but committed individuals pursuing political change through violence remain the menace most likely to strike the homeland and its interests abroad.[1] Given the immediate and persistent nature of this threat, it is important to understand how violent extremism spreads in the hopes of future containment. For these reasons, the concept of radicalization is gaining ever more attention as counterterrorism experts struggle to address an increasingly complex and diffuse threat in an efficient and effective fashion. Radicalization, in the context of this paper, is defined as the process by which people come to adopt extremist political beliefs with a particular emphasis on those ideologies that encourage violent action.[2]

A central impediment to policy, strategy and tactics focused on curtailing radicalization lies in the complexity of a phenomenon that has thus far belied efforts to explain or predict outcomes. For all the attention that curtailing radicalization has attracted, the predominant approach to policy design emphasizes the risks inherent in exposure to radical ideas. The resulting policies aim to reduce exposure to radical material in physical locations like prisons or virtual arenas like chat rooms, but limited understanding of radicalization challenges further policy development. In short, there is a need for more scientific study of radicalization that builds on a knowledge disbursed among different disciplines that rarely cross paths. This project, focused on the coevolutionary nature of social and ideological radicalization forces, is not meant as a decisive work, but instead a step toward the creative application of theory and empirics in a modest scientific exploration of radicalization.

This study argues that the spread of violent extremism cannot be fully understood as an ideological or social phenomenon, but must be viewed as a process that integrates the two forces in a coevolutionary manner. The same forces that make an ideology

---

[1] While the current terrorist threat may not present an existential threat to survival, the possibility of WMD terrorism does raise the stakes considerably. Such an attack, while not a challenge to U.S. existence, might well have significant consequences for domestic and foreign security policy.

[2] There are numerous ways that one could define radicalization, with one of the most important distinctions being the difference between violent and non-violent radicals. This paper will use the definition above, though this an area worthy of further exploration itself.

appealing to some aggrieved group of people are not necessarily the same factors that promote its transfer through social networks of self-interested human beings. This means that there is value in differentiating between why radical ideologies resonate among individuals, and how those individuals come to adopt and pass on those ideas.

As a result, radicalization inexorably intertwines social and ideological forces in systemic fashion. The coevolutionary nature of the social and ideological spheres presents a unique challenge and is one of the reasons that rigorous efforts to identify a radical or terrorist profile have not yielded significant return. Efforts to develop an archetype often focuses on individual traits, but it may be that profiles based on social and ideological behavior need to be considered simultaneously in developing a theory that is actionable for counterterrorism practitioners.

Radicalization and violent mobilization, as represented in an integrative framework here, is a four stage process whereby individuals become aware of a radical ideology, find themselves interested in the doctrine and come to accept the extremist beliefs and norms. In a fourth stage, violent radicals then act on the norm set and implement violence. This process addresses how radicalization occurs rather than why. The prototypical radical will progress through each of these stages. People may also skip one or more stages or backslide, generating feedback loops that either erode or reinforce interest in radical ideas. The process is sufficiently general to apply across radical ideologies without focusing on any single ideological doctrine, but the empirics in the study focus on jihadist terror cells. A central argument advanced here is that the nature of progression through these different stages is not uniform, and therefore the patterns and effects of social ties vary as people build their experience of radicalism.

There are a series of conclusions that follow empirical analyses of radicalization and terrorist behavior. First, the fear of lone wolf radical jihadists, those who implement violence while lacking any relationships to other extremists, has not yet materialized in any broad fashion. There is a persistent belief that young men will emerge violently from their basements after spending hours viewing global militant jihadist material, but the historical record provides little evidence of true lone wolves in pursuit of global jihad. There appears to be a strong social component whereby the vast majority of people reach out in search of social ties and validation before taking action, and the changing nature of online social activity offers greater opportunity to make those connections from the basement than ever before. This does not necessarily increase the likelihood of lone wolf global jihadism, since these individuals cease to be lone wolves once they become part of the social community be it physical or virtual. It does, however, increase the likelihood that future attacks nurtured in this online social environment have certain characteristics like planning cycles that resemble those common to lone wolf incidents.

Second, social ties play a critical role in radicalization, and there are important nonlinear but systemic patterns in social trajectories. Radicals affiliated with attack networks tend to form social relationships in a nonlinear fashion, gradually increasing the number of new individuals they encounter early on, and then forming fewer new connections over time. This pattern of social behavior parallels the barriers to entry as people proceed down the radical path, in which social ties prove most important in the acceptance stage. There is also a nonlinear relationship between ideological affinity and social ties that challenges conventional wisdom. One might think that social ties are more important for recruiting those with less ideological affinity. Analysis shows that social relationships are equally important for both the high and low affinity individuals, and somewhat less so for those in the middle. Systemic nonlinearity in social trajectories means that opportunities for intervention exist in specific places that may not be fully appreciated.

Third, there are also common patterns in the social structure of terrorist cells assessed here, offering insights into the social and ideological regulatory patterns of these groups. Like most social networks, there are a few highly powered individuals who can play the role of super brokers, those connected to well-connected people across different subgroups, and market makers, those closely connected to others capable of spanning subgroups. One important aspect common to many radical groups is that they display high levels of closeness, meaning that many people are well-situated to facilitate the flow between members and monitor activity. Many members are capable of communicating or observing others easily despite the absence of very-well-connected individuals. These patterns of interconnectivity present both strengths and weaknesses for radical groups and the radicalization process.

Fourth, the concept of recruitment receives much attention, but it may not function as envisioned by conventional wisdom. The majority of individuals who participate in violent cells are first brought into their social network by others who will bring in one, two or three people. Those who bring in five or more participants are actually responsible for connecting a relatively low percentage of participants. While there is great variation in the structure and operation of terrorist groups, the analysis here suggests that recruitment is more a natural social process with many individuals organically developing a network rather than the purview of a few individuals hierarchically tasked to do so. Every member has the potential to spread the group's ideology to others, and they may in fact have self-serving reasons for doing so. There is an understandably strong emphasis on ideological motivations in studying the spread of violent extremism, but individual participants can actually improve their social standing and group power by bringing in new members. Recruitment is a utilitarian activity and not simply an ideological imperative.

There are some important limitations to the research described here, as with any study. The analysis focuses on the social aspects of radicalization and relies heavily on some basic yet powerful social network tools. As a result, the analysis and conclusions focus heavily on those insights, but there is much more work that could be done relying on narrative analysis, process tracing, experiments or other techniques. The social network analysis is also done using the small sample of cases from the John Jay and Artis dataset simply because this is the only data available that shows the changes in terrorist social networks over time. While the sample is small, analyses leveraging this data appeared in leading political violence peer-reviewed publications.[3] These offer a deeper discussion of the strengths and weaknesses of the dataset. Despite these shortcomings, the insights provided here can hopefully serve as a launching pad for points of debate in larger scientific and policy discussions about radicalization.

The next section of the paper proceeds to review some of the prior material on radicalization and offers a simple model. The review is not meant to be comprehensive, especially considering the diffusion of knowledge across multiple disciplines, but instead highlights some specific insights derived from social, behavioral and biological sciences that serve as a foundation for the project.

---

[3] Justin Magourick, Scott Atran and Marc Sageman, "Connecting Terrorist Networks," *Studies in Conflict & Terrorism* 31 no. 1 (2008), 1–16; and Scott Helfstein and Dominick Wright, "Covert or Convenient? Evolution of Terror Attack Networks," *Journal of Conflict Resolution* (March 2011).

This is followed by a section that steps back to consider the importance of social relationships by looking across a data set of American jihadist plots and focuses closely on the lone wolf incidents. Results suggest that social processes play a critically important role. The third main section then introduces some concepts from social network analysis and applies them to look for empirical patterns. These concepts are utilized in the fourth section to examine the social trajectory of new members and the process by which people are socialized into a cell. The fifth section explores how individual social roles can impact cell functions by considering a range of network typologies. The final main section then looks at the individuals responsible for serving as a gateway for extremism or recruiting new members. The paper concludes with a series of implications.

Radicalization is an important aspect of political violence, and one that research has traditionally struggled to explain. Scholars and practitioners draw from a diverse set of theoretical approaches with particular emphasis on social mobilization theory, biographical explanations and psychological exposition. Recognizing that the complex phenomenon of radicalization draws on a series of factors, some efforts aim at integrating these different approaches in a holistic fashion. This process begins by surveying some of the different approaches and explanations focused on why some people radicalize, and then looks at the processes of how radicalization occurs. This provides the foundation to explore the relationship between the processes of individual radicalization and group formation in more detail.

Some of the best insights come from the social movement literature, and specifically that which deals with mobilization for high-risk activity.[4] Doug McAdam, in his seminal study of participants in the 1964 Freedom Summer project aimed at promoting voting rights in Mississippi, proposed a model of mobilization that draws an important distinction between low- and high-risk activity.[5] He proposes that low-risk activity is conditioned on receptive political attitudes, formed through familial or social influences and contact with activists. Attitudes and contact may drive people to flirt with low-risk activism even if they are not necessarily committed. The barriers to entry for high-risk activity are far greater, requiring further conditioning. McAdam proposes that the escalation to high-risk activism is a circular process whereby participation increases association with the activist network, in turn deepening ideological socialization, further fostering an ideological identity and ultimately increasing the likelihood of high risk activism. This process is either advanced or hindered by biographical availability, which captures the notion that people with alternative priorities such as families and jobs are less likely to find themselves in this cycle.

The theory on high-risk activism finds empirical support in the Freedom Summer dataset where it was tested by comparing actual participants versus individuals that withdrew, with some factors proving stronger than others. Those who were already

---

[4] Sidney Tarrow, *Power in Movement: Social Movements and Contentious Politics* (Cambridge, UK: Cambridge University Press, 2011).

[5] Doug McAdam, "Recruitment to High-Risk Activism: The Case of Freedom Summer," *American Journal of Sociology* 92, no. 1 (July 1986), 64–90.

active in political organizations and enjoyed stronger social ties with other group members were less likely to withdraw from the program, offering strong support for the importance of participation and sociological connections. There was modest support for the importance of attitude and affinity, but it did not hold across all the different measurements. Biographical availability was not a particularly strong predictor with modest support as well, but there is an important caveat to the findings particularly pertinent for attitudinal affinity and biographical availability. All of the subjects, both those who participated and those who withdrew, signed up to participate and thereby selected into the study group. As a result, the study does not include a sample of those who opted out to begin with, and cannot be used to identify whether attitudinal or biographical differences exist between those that self-selected into the sample and the rest of the population.[6] McAdam does note that there appears to be a predisposition for joining high-risk activism at a time when young individuals assert their independence and may as result see these activities as a means of enhancing their status, but it remains difficult to draw further conclusions on biographical availability.[7]

This early work on high-risk mobilization proves a useful baseline to build upon and from which to evaluate more recent and similarly rigorous work on radicalization, which remains in short supply despite the widespread interest in the subject. Many

---

[6] The McAdam study is analogous to examining 300 individuals that go for terrorist training, where 100 participate in terrorist activities and 200 do not. A study of those 300 individuals may yield attitudinal and biographical insights into the differences between these groups but says little about factors that may or may not differentiate these 300 who pursued training from the rest of the population that did not.

[7] The argument linking poverty to terrorism remains an important part of the discourse, but repeated work on community-wide economic metrics like unemployment and terrorist violence show they have no relationship. This raises legitimate questions about the efficacy of reducing terrorism and political violence through unemployment rates, but it suffers from data limitations that result in aggregate rather individual analysis. There remains insufficient data on the individual level to test the hypothesis whether employed people are more likely to engage in terrorism or political violence. It is interesting to note that many members of al-Qaʿida and individuals participating in domestic plots often have families, high employment prospects and jobs. For studies on terrorism and poverty see James A. Piazza, "Rooted in Poverty? Terrorism, Poor Economic Development, and Social Cleavages," *Terrorism and Political Violence* 18, no. 1 (2006), 159–177; Alberto Abadie, "Poverty, Political Freedom, and the Roots of Terrorism," *American Economic Review* 96 no. 2 (2006), 50–56. Another interesting example is Eli Berman, Michael Callen, Joseph H. Felter and Jacob N. Shapiro, "Do Working Men Rebel? Insurgency and Unemployment in Iraq and the Philippines," (NBER Working Paper No. 15547, 2009). It is important to note that this project better reflects aggregate trends between unemployment and political violence as the data analysis cannot actually assess whether those who were actually unemployed were more or less likely to join an insurgency.

studies in radicalization focus on what McAdams calls "personalogical" factors, often defined or characterized by individual traits that contribute to radicalization. Unfortunately, this approach is yet to offer a robust theory or empirical explanation of extremist tendencies. Jeff Victoroff did an extensive survey of this work to understand its strengths and limitations, finding little evidence to suggest that terrorists are psychotic or suffer from personality disorders.[8] There are, however, reasons to believe that psychological explanations such as identity theory, sociological concepts like frustration-aggression or certain cognitive biases may offer greater insights to personalogical studies.[9]

It is reasonable to imagine that there exists some set of personal or psychological traits common among the tiny minority of individuals engaged in terrorist activity that lowers the threshold for radicalization. Different cognitive or psychological elements may well be salient for individuals across different groups, meaning there is no single type but a series of types depending on group affiliation. While some studies try to engage these issues based on available data, there is a lack of hypothesis testing using validated methodology and controlled experiments.[10] Available data suggest there may exist certain cognitive or psychological aspects common to terrorists, and one may well imagine that there are commonalities among those who engage in this relatively rare behavior, the sum of the available empirical data is too weak to draw systemic conclusions on personalogical and psychological factors.

---

[8] Jeff Victoroff, "The Mind of the Terrorist: A Review and Critique of Psychological Approaches," *Journal of Conflict Resolution* 49, no. 3 (February 2005), 3–42. Note that psychotic is defined as an Axis I clinical disorder that often implies loss of reality whereby people do not know right from wrong, whereas personality disorders are considered an Axis II condition.

[9] One of the few data driven studies is Michel Gottschalk and Simon Gottschalk, "Authoritarianism and pathological hatred: A social psychological profile of the middle eastern terrorist," *The American Sociologist* 35, no. 2 (2004), 38–59. They do find systemic commonalities across MMPI tests administered to 90 jailed terrorists that highlight tendencies toward authoritarianism and pathological hatred, but there is much more data collection needed to confirm these assessments.

[10] For demographic and criminological approaches see Jerome P. Bjelopera and Mark A. Randol, *American Jihadist Terrorism: Combating a Complex Threat* (Washington, DC: Congressional Research Service, September 20, 2010); Brian Michael Jenkins, *Would-Be Warriors: Incidents of Jihadist Terrorist Radicalization in the United States Since September 11, 2001* (Washington, DC: RAND Occasional Paper, 2010); and Peter Bergen and Bruce Hoffman, *Assessing the Terrorist Threat* (Washington, DC: Bipartisan Policy Center, 2010).

One attempt to extend the personalogical approach and explain why young people join al-Qaʿida relies on "seeking" behavior. By focusing on individual needs and emphazing the importance of individual motive, Mark Venhaus moves beyond typical personal profiles without generating an unwieldy framework.[11] Al-Qaʿida recruits, in his extensive sample, can be characterized by four motivational profiles: revenge seekers, thrill seekers, identity seekers and status seekers. Revenge seekers and thrill seekers are fairly straightforward. Identity seekers look to build a sense of self that is tied to their group participation, and status seekers desire recognition for their action. These four motives offer a powerful and simple way to explain why people engage with al-Qaʿida, and also suggest ways of diverting each seeking type. While the work offers an interesting explanation of why people engage with al-Qaʿida, it does not really capture the process by which it occurs, or, in other words, how it comes to happen.

John Horgan's seminal work on deradicalization and demobilization in the Northern Ireland conflict emphasizes the importance of processes.[12] Horgan begins by engaging the personalogical approach, but argues that study of pathways offers a better approach for understanding radical behavior than the study of profiles does. He identifies three stages of radical engagement: becoming involved, being involved and disengaging. The factors that may matter or promote radical behavior in one stage might not be the same as in other stages. For example, the reasons someone stays engaged may not be the same factors that drove his or her initial involvement. This distinction between factors at different stages becomes critical in the study of disengagement, since removing the forces that instigated and sustained radical behavior might not generate the desired behavior change. The process of facilitating disengagement needs to focus on aspects pertinent to that stage. While elucidating the importance of pathways, Horgan stops short of providing a framework explaining the process of becoming involved or radicalization and mobilization.

At the same time as focusing on process, Horgan also specifies a series of factors that may predispose someone to pursue terrorism: emotional vulnerability, dissatisfaction

---

[11] John M. Venhaus, *Special Report: Why Youth Join al-Qaeda* (Washington, DC: United States Institute of Peace, 2010).

[12] John Horgan, "From Profiles to Pathways and Roots to Routes: Perspectives from Psychology on Radicalization into Terrorism," *The ANNALS of the American Academy of Political and Social Science* 618 (2008), 80–94; John Horgan, *Walking Away From Terrorism: Accounts of Disengagement from Radical and Extremist Movements* (New York, NY: Taylor & Francis, 2009).

with his or her current activity, sense of victimization, belief that engaging in violence is not immoral, belief in possible reward and social connections to violent individuals.[13] One might argue that radicalization at its core is the process by which people come to believe that violence in pursuit of their objective is not immoral. This is a crucial aspect of political violence, both among its perpetrators and supporters. While simplifying a complicated concept, Horgan helps to highlight the difference between why people radicalize and how people radicalize. The causes behind the pursuit of terrorism may be somewhat different from the process of radicalization, despite some important overlaps. This begs the question of how people reach the point at which terrorism becomes an acceptable course of action.

Social and behavioral sciences have stressed the importance of processes and stages in radicalization, and this project attempts to leverage, integrate and build upon those insights. Rather than elucidate a framework aimed at identifying the causes of radicalization, this project focuses on the individual processes through which people progress and the way individual journeys, ideologies and group dynamics synergize to foster violence.[14]

Scholars have offered and tested an array of radicalization models with modest differences in the number and type of stages, which is captured here in a four-step process of awareness, interest, acceptance and implementation.[15] Each requires brief definition.

The first stage involves initial exposure to radical ideas. Awareness can be thought of in two distinct ways. The first is a binary function in which people are either aware or unaware. In this case, once someone is made aware of a radical doctrine, it is almost impossible to become unaware or to unlearn that information. An alternative notion of

---

[13] Ibid.

[14] Gary Robins, "Understanding individual behaviors within covert networks: The interplay of individual qualities, psychological predispositions, and network effects," *Trends in Organized Crime* 12 (2009), 166–187.

[15] This is simpler than some other efforts such as that outlined by Horgan or that found in Clark McCauley and Sophia Moskalenko, "Mechanisms of Political Radicalization: Pathways Toward Terrorism," *Terrorism and Political Violence* 20, no. 3 (July 2008), 415–433. Many complex models tend toward blending the motivations or justifications for violence with the process by which people come to adopt those explanations. The simple model focuses only process without focus on justification or motivation.

awareness is continuous in nature and views awareness as a gradual process that occurs over time. People may move back and forth through the awareness as they learn more, but it is important to note that awareness is a precursor to any other stage of radicalization. People will likely move to other stages once they acquire sufficient information, and the threshold on sufficiency is likely to differ across individuals. One person may have a relatively low threshold, meaning they are immediately interested in the radical goals and methods associated with the doctrine, while others may require far more familiarity before the ideas begin to seem compelling.

Once an individual is aware of radical ideas, he or she must decide whether these ideas are of interest to him or her or to dismiss them as noise. "Interest" in this sense is deeper than knowledge or intellectual curiosity. Many people explore areas they have little interest in pursuing to great depth. In this sense, "interest" has a deeper normative connotation that involves an individual's belief system. Individuals who lack interest may quickly turn away after becoming aware of radical ideas. This notion of interest involves the willingness to alter one's belief system or social norms to reflect those associated with an ideological doctrine. This distinguishes those casual observers with intellectual curiosity from those who find deeper meaning in the radical ideas.

Those interested in the radical ideas then progress to acceptance, whereby they come to adopt the beliefs and social norms expressed in the radical ideology. Acceptance is often a crucial precursor to violent action, since as Horgan highlights, people must first believe that the use of violence in pursuit of a cause is not immoral before they will actually attempt any action. Once someone accepts the radical ideology, they are primed to conduct violence. It is important to note, however, that many radicals never actually conduct violence, making it important to distinguish violent radicals from other radicals. One might argue that the difference between violent and nonviolent radicals is that the former act on their beliefs while the later fail to do so. This is plausible, but one might also argue that difference actually occurs sooner, in the acceptance stage. For example, there are belief systems that advocate for a global Islamist Caliphate but eschew violence as a means to achieve that goal. This is a stark contrast from al-Qa`ida's vision of achieving a global caliphate through violence. The difference, as envisioned here, is that the individual who adopts the nonviolent approach has accepted a fundamentally different set of norms than the individual who pursues violence. This means that there is a distinction between those who adopt radical doctrines, those who adopt violent radical doctrines, and those who conduct terrorist acts in accordance with radical violent doctrines.

A simple model of radicalization would propose that stages take place sequentially, but empirical evidence from radicalized individuals does not support a strictly linear process.[16] Radicalization is often iterative, with feedback loops that reinforce radical ideas or backslides that move people away from violent action. Complicating matters further, there are exceptional cases whereby people bypass stages, perhaps going directly from awareness or interest to implementation. These instances are usually marked by a shallow understanding of ideology or a radical ideology that sits alongside preexisting counterculture tendencies or illness. For example, the perpetrator of the 2006 vehicle attack in Chapel Hill, North Carolina, Mohammed Reza Taheri-azar, referenced al-Qa`ida's ideology as part of his justification, but he also had a history of disruptive and countercultural behavior.[17] It is not at all clear that he truly came adopt the beliefs and social norms that undergird militant global jihadism rather than simply the violent extroversion of its belief system. It is important that an accurate model be able to capture these different possible permutations.

The complete framework for the individual process is reflected in Figure 1, with arrows indicating the paths people may take as they radicalize. The linear path, whereby people move from left to right following the solid arrows, is the most straightforward. The hollow arrows represent alternative possible routes. As people progress, they may find themselves acquiring new information that pushes them backward down the path. In fact, many people may become aware and interested, but fail to reach the acceptance stage without greater exposure to new information and social relationships. These feedback loops may ultimately help radicalize individuals and allow them to build deep understanding and faith in the principles, but they can also offer opportunities for disrupting the process as interested parties continue reaching out to build awareness. Intervention in the searching process associated with awareness and interest might

---

[16] For example, the staircase metaphor articulated by Fathali Moghaddam might allow for people to move back and forth between "floors," but that is never made explicit and makes the framework seem linear. See Fathali M. Moghaddam, "The Staircase to Terrorism: A Psychological Exploration," *American Psychologist* 60, no. 2 (Feb/Mar 2005), 161–169.

[17] Jane Stancill and Jessica Rocha, "Taheri-azar Expects Life in Prison," *News & Observer* 16 March 2006. The stabbing of a parliament member from the United Kingdom, Stephen Timms, is an interesting example of a rapidly activated lone wolf outside of the U.S. context.

seem the easiest approach, since people are just beginning down the path, but the scale of effort needed to be successful would be quite large given the number of people that become aware. For the people moving down the path, the searching associated with awareness and interest are also the easiest stages to move through since the barriers to entry are relatively low.

Figure 1: Radicalization Process

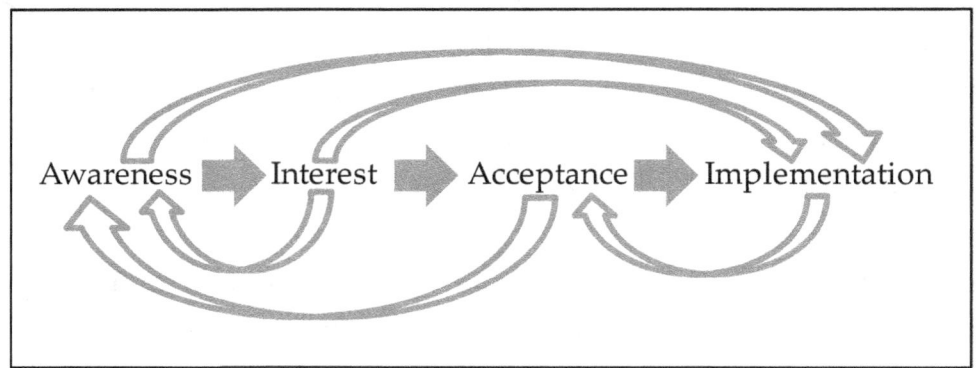

This radicalization process encompasses a variety of paths, including the basic linear process and one involving feedback loops, and it also acknowledges that some people jump across certain stages. An example of the first might take the form of someone made aware of radical ideas and immediately implementing them without really internalizing their beliefs and norms. Charles Bishop, the young man who flew a small plane into an office building in Tampa, Florida, in 2002, represents one such example.[18] Similarly, one might move from awareness to interest and then perpetrate violence without going through the acceptance stage. Leaps such as this characterize unique challenges to basic models of the radicalization process as well as any outside efforts to intervene on a practical or tactical level. Since radicalization often takes time, there may be opportunity to interrupt the process. When individuals skip stages, intervention becomes all the more difficult.

The barriers to entry across stages vary considerably. The barriers to awareness are particularly low, then likely increase in the interest stage. As one moves down the path, it may be most difficult to transverse the border between interest and acceptance. This challenge is well documented by jihadist strategists and recruiting documents. Much of

---

[18] Deborah Sharp, "Teen Had 'Sympathy' for Bin Laden," *USA Today* 7 January 2002.

the propaganda material produced by radicals specifically targets this transition.[19] Once someone truly adopts the radical worldview, the step toward violence may be somewhat easier if it is explicitly part of that doctrine. This predicts a curvilinear relationship between the stages of radicalization and the barriers to entry across them. Costs, in this case the difficulty associated with radicalization, increase as people move through awareness, interest and most importantly acceptance, then likely decline as people move from acceptance to implementation. This would be consistent with studies that indicate the integrative complexity of world leaders tends to decline after they have made the decision to engage in military activity.[20] Once they believe that their interests are best served by violence (a moment analogous to the acceptance stage), there is a tendency to reduce cognitive dissonance that may well make the violent course appear as the easier or more appealing option.

As McAdam, Horgan and others note, it is difficult to identify a profile that successfully predicts an individual's likelihood of proceeding through the stages of radicalization. While personalogical approaches remain constrained by limits of data and methods of systemic assessment, the research on high-risk mobilization finds strong evidence that social networks affect the likelihood of participation in radical activities.[21] This might drive one to wonder whether social relationships similarly affect the radicalization process and, if so, what role they play. One might posit that radicalization involves different stages or processes, but this basic construct serves as a tool to evaluate the relationship between individual and group dynamics.

The importance of social interaction will vary across the stages of radicalization as well as the motives for joining radical groups as specified by Venhaus.[22] Social interaction may play little or no role in the awareness stage, where individuals first learn of a radical ideology. Given the explosion of readily accessible radical material and the in-

---

[19] Abu-Amr al-Qa'idi, "A Course in the Art of Recruiting Mujahidin," posted to Jihadi Forum on 7 September 2008.

[20] Peter Suedfeld and Philip E. Tetlock, "War, Peace, and Integrative Complexity: UN Speeches on the Middle East Problem, 1947–1976," *Journal of Conflict Resolution* 21, no. 3 (September 1977), 427–442; and Peter Suedfeld and Susan Bluck, "Changes in Integrative Complexity prior to Surprise Attacks," *Journal of Conflict Resolution* 32, no. 4 (Dec. 1988), 626–635.

[21] See McAdam (1986); and Karl-Dieter Opp and Christiane Gern, "Dissident Groups, Personal Networks, and Spontaneous Cooperation: The East German Revolution of 1989," *American Sociological Review* 58, no. 5 (October 1993), 659–680.

[22] Venhaus (2010).

depth news coverage of terrorism incidents, it is not difficult to encounter or obtain material from any number of radical groups. Awareness may come about through push media, such as television news broadcasts, or pull sources such as the Internet. That is to say, some people may actively seek radical content, but many others may be exposed to it by accident. While awareness need not be tied to social relationships, such ties do offer another avenue by which people may first come to encounter radical ideology.

Awareness itself has been proved a poor predictor of behavior. Mass media or messaging campaigns often help to spread information, but studies indicate that very few people change behavior based on new information alone.[23] The behavior of others in an individual's social network acts as a far better predictor of his or her behavior change and adoption. Studies of health programs show how behavioral changes of others in a social network can exert significant influence over subsequent action.[24] While the affect of social relationships may be limited in the awareness stage, they can be crucial as people continue down the pathway towards radical activity. In that sense, social interaction may play an indirect function early in the process by facilitating a quicker or easier transition to later stages. It may also help to prevent backsliding, as individuals introduced to a radicalism through interpersonal relationships may have trouble disengaging because of peer pressure or changes to social status.

As people progress past awareness into the interest stage, motivations come to interact with social ties in some important ways. Those motivated by revenge or thrill-seeking behavior may not care about interaction with those around them. By contrast, those interested in the identity or status associated with involvement in a radical group will be deeply influenced by personal relationships and social ties during this time.[25] Both

---

[23] It is important to distinguish between two different elements of influence. In voting behavior, for example, campaigns may not motivate an individual to vote, but it may influence the direction of a vote. Paul F. Lazarsfeld, Bernard Berelson and Hazel Gaudet, *The People's Choice: How the Voter Makes Up His Mind in a Presidential Campaign* (New York, NY: Columbia University Press, 1948).

[24] Catherine Campbell and Zodwa Mzaidume, "Grassroots Participation, Peer Education, and HIV Prevention by Sex Workers in South Africa," *American Journal of Public Health* 91, no. 12 (December 2001), 1978–1986; Albert Bandura, "Health Promotion by Social Cognitive Means," *Health Education Behavior* 31, no. 2 (April 2004), 143–164. See reviews such as I. H. Yen and S. Leonard Syme, "The Social Environment and Health: A Discussion of the Epidemiologic Literature," *Annual Review of Public Health* 20 (1999), 287–308; and Sonya Grier and Carol A. Bryant, "Social Marketing in Public Health," *Annual Review of Public Health* 26 (2005), 319–339.

[25] These distinctions may not prove pertinent if it is impossible to distinguish between these different types of seekers and the resulting implications for their radicalization process. If, however, behavioral

identity and status are inherently social processes. The former is usually rooted in a group, and identity theory stresses the importance of association with members.[26] Status is also a social characteristic, since it relies on improving one's image in the eyes of others. Without social interactions, identity seekers would never come to associate with group members and status seekers would have no audience whereby they can improve their position. While those interested in revenge or excitement can progress through the interest stage with little social interaction, these ties are critical for ensuring that that the identity and status seekers can actually accommodate the motivations that drive their interest.

It would seem that the stage where personalogical approaches really struggle to explain radicalization is in the acceptance stage, where arguably social relationships prove most crucial. Victoroff notes a series of psychological and cognitive traits that may increase the propensity to join radical groups, but systemic research has shown that many extremists have fairly ordinary personality profiles.[27] McAdam's argument is that social relationships are a defining difference between those who indicate interest in higher-risk activism versus those who actually participate.[28] In terrorism research, this theme is advanced by Justin Magourick, Scott Atran and Marc Sageman, who argue that kinship and social connections prove the best determinant of individual involvement.[29] Similar to this study, their research focuses on those who actually participate in terrorist activity, but as result does not capture or account for the large numbers of individuals in kinship networks who fail to participate in terrorism.

While there is sufficient empirical precedent for advancing an argument based on the importance of social relationships in the acceptance stage, it also worth elucidating some of the social and cognitive mechanisms that facilitate this process. Radical ideologies fundamentally offer a set of social norms, or acceptable standards of

---

profiles can be developed between those engaged in high-risk leisure activities from those interested in group prestige, then there may be opportunity to observe different trajectories and adjust interventions.

[26] Seth J. Schwartz, Curtis S. Dunkel and Alan S. Waterman, "Terrorism: An Identity Theory Perspective," *Studies on Conflict and Terrorism* 32, no. 6 (2009), 537–559.

[27] Victoroff (2005).

[28] McAdam (1986).

[29] Justin Magourick, Scott Atran and Marc Sageman, "Connecting Terrorist Networks," *Studies in Conflict & Terrorism* 31, no. 1 (2008), 1–16.

behavior, that run contrary to those found elsewhere in society.[30] The evolution of norms is a social or communal process, as there must be a center of gravity that puts forth the radical ideas as an acceptable or even preferable alternative.[31] The process of an individual's adopting norms is often tied to the behavior of those nearby, and Robert Axelrod describes different ways that societies can sustain norms.[32] One common method is through punishment, either of the violator or those who observe violations and fail to punish in response. Without such social pressures and the risk of punishment, it may be difficult to sustain commitment to radical ideals. Collective action work specifically examines how people overcome constraints to action, and Elinor Ostrom argues that it is crucial for interested individuals to send signals and design institutions to encourage cooperation.[33] Communication and social processes play a central role. It is possible for individuals to adopt norms without social reinforcement, but the barriers to entry increase significantly.

There is also a strong tendency toward in-group and out-group behavior that may foster acceptance. Research shows that individuals assigned to teams come to sympathize with in-group members and show enmity to out-group members very quickly, even if the distinctions are essentially fictional and the members have had no prior contact.[34] Feelings of disgust, which may prove critical in the psychological sanctioning of violence, are deeply tied to in-group and out-group dynamics.[35] There is a much greater tendency to view members of the out-group with disgust, making it easier to perpetrate violence against them. This sense of in-group is often socially constructed through interaction with other group members and shared grievance

---

[30] Russell Hardin, "The Crippled Epistemology of Extremism," *Political Extremism and Rationality*, edited by A. Breton, G. Galeotti, P. Salmon and R. Wintrobe (New York, NY: Cambridge University Press, 2002), 3–22.

[31] Edward L. Glaeser and Cass R. Sunstein, "Extremism and Social Learning," (NBER Working Paper No. 13687, 2007).

[32] Robert Axelrod, "An Evolutionary Approach to Norms," *American Political Science Review* 80, no. 4 (December 1986), 1095–1111.

[33] Elinor Ostrom, "Collective Action and the Evolution of Social Norms," *Journal of Economic Perspectives* 14, no. 3 (Summer 2000), 137–158.

[34] John W. Howard and Myron Rothbart, "Social Categorization and Memory for In-Group and Out-Group Behavior," *Journal of Personality and Social Psychology* 38, no. 2 (Feb 1980), 301–310.

[35] David Matsumoto, "Cultural Similarities and Differences in Display Rules," *Motivation and Emotion* 14, no. 3 (1990), 195–214; and Lasana T. Harris and Susan T. Fiske, "Dehumanizing the Lowest of the Low: Neuroimaging Responses to Extreme Out-Groups," *Psychological Science* 17, no. 10 (October 2006), 847–853.

toward out-group members. Lasana Harris and Susan Fiske have shown that these differential responses actually tie to differences in neurobiological function and are not simply behavioral observations or manifestations.[36] For example, research subjects shown pictures of people from out-groups display reduced neural activity in parts of the brain associated with empathy or attributing other's thoughts. Emile Bruneau and Rebecca Saxe found that activity in a specific part of the brain, the precuneus, correlated with participants' attitudes to the Israeli-Arab conflict, again highlighting the deep-rooted nature of certain social groupings or distinctions.[37]

Anecdotal evidence from Internet activity across fringe groups compliments these social and neurobiological studies highlighting the power of groups in norm development, attitude and behavior. The Internet offers people a medium by which they can build communities with others they might come into contact with in the course of ordinary life.[38] This offers people the opportunity to discover new belief and norm sets while simultaneously presenting the possibility for social interaction with group members who can reinforce these norms. Over the past decade, there have been a number of examples of the spread of violent extremism through the Internet. Taken together, they form an example of a situation where a small subset of the population may have an interest in activities most reject and may never do anything in pursuit of these interests until they find a similarly inclined community that validates such behavior. This extends to other illicit behavior as well.

Finding a community of like-minded individuals becomes a critical part of abandoning social norms and adopting those of a fringe population. To be sure, there are those "de-norm" entrepreneurs, individuals bound to deconstruct social norms who will operate without social support, but they would seem to be the farthest tails of the population distribution or the outliers of the outlying population. In a similar sense, Major Nidal Hassan, the Fort Hood shooter, may never have come into contact with Anwar al-Alawki's writings nor attempted to reach out and build a social tie in search of

---

[36] Lasana T. Harris and Susan T. Fiske, "Social Groups that Elicit Disgust are Differentially Processed in mPFC," *Social Cognitive & Affective Neuroscience* 2, no. 1 (2007), 45–51.

[37] Emile G. Bruneau and Rebecca Saxe, "Attitudes Towards the Outgroup are Predicted by Activity in the Precuneus in Arabs and Israelis," *NeuroImage* 52, no. 4 (October 2010), 1704–1711.

[38] Eileen Fischer, Julia Bristor and Brenda Gainer, "Creating or Escaping Community? An Explanatory Study of Internet Consumers' Behaviors," *Advances in Consumer Research* 23 (1996), 178–182.

validation for his worldview if not for the ease of online activity.[39] While some might question the value of online correspondence and social networking tools, early research offers reasons to give such relationships serious consideration. Paul Zak finds that the receipt of a properly worded Twitter message can release as much oxytocin (a hormone critical to bonding and trust) as seeing a loved one walk into a room.[40]

Adopting new beliefs or norms in the acceptance stage has a strong social component, but implementation of these beliefs need not rely as strongly on such interaction. Should the newly adopted belief system stress communal violence or uprising, then social ties will continue to play a key role. Ideologies that stress the importance of individual imperative reduce the importance of social connections, though they may fail to eliminate the social aspect of the action altogether.[41] In other words, people who truly come to accept the individualist global militant jihadist ideological doctrine may well find further social behavior unnecessary since they are already primed for violence.[42]

It is important to point out that social relationships may play less of a role in implementation than acceptance, but they are by no means inconsequential. Social relationships can and do play a variety of functions in the violent stage. First, they may offer individuals access to capabilities otherwise not available. Groups of people are often better at solving complex tasks, capable of simultaneously carrying out parallel activities and may offer access to specific skills like bomb making.[43] Second, social ties may help to prevent backsliding and second thoughts prior to violent action through negative reinforcement like peer pressure or positive inducement like camaraderie.[44] These functional advantages of social ties during implementation may be offset by

---

[39] Jenkins (2010). Admittedly, Alawki's works were widely available in bookstores prior to 2008, and that may have offered another avenue to access the material.

[40] Adam L. Penenberg, "Social Networking Affects Brains Like Falling in Love," *Fast Company* 1 July 2010.

[41] Al-Qa`ida's brand of radical ideology specifically calls for individual imperative in violent struggle; for more, see Nelly Lahoud, *The Jihadis' Path to Self-Destruction* (New York, NY: Columbia University Press, 2010).

[42] Examples of individual calls for jihad are exemplified by material in *Inspire* magazine and statements such as that found on al-Shumkuh, http://117.102.253.146/~shamikh/vb/showthread.php?t=136406, accessed 21 November 2011.

[43] Ken Kollman, John H. Miller and Scott E. Page, "Decentralization and Search for Policy Solutions," *Journal of Law Economics and Organization* 16, no. 1 (2000), 202–228.

[44] Martha Crenshaw, "Explaining Suicide Terrorism: A Review Essay," *Security Studies* 16, no. 1 (January 2007), 133–162.

utilitarian disadvantage. For example, making new social relationships in the implementation stage may increase the likelihood that the cell is penetrated by counterterrorism professionals.[45] Social relationships will often continue to play important roles in implementation, but perhaps not as significant as is in the prior acceptance stage.

The relationship elucidated in the prior paragraphs leads to the first of two hypotheses pertaining to radicalization and social interaction referred to as the Social-Stage hypothesis. Mobilization literature stresses the importance of social relationships and group involvement, arguing that it is crucially important for involvement in high-risk activism.[46] This does not satisfactorily articulate how the importance of such relationships changes over time. Similarly, terrorism radicalization literature using personalogical approaches has not explicitly considered the variable role of social relationships in the propensity for radicalization at different stages in the pathway. Without clear justification, there is no reason to believe that the value of such relationships changes over time.

The Social-Stage hypothesis put forth here argues that there is variation in the importance of relationships through the stages of radicalization, and this differential is nonlinear in nature. Social relationships are least important in the earliest stage of awareness, and become more important in the interest stage. They are subsequently most important when individuals come to the acceptance stage but then decline in implementation. This relationship is displayed in Figure 2, where the null hypothesis predicts that radicalizing individuals are likely to develop new relationships at a consistent rate over time. The Social-Stage hypothesis predicts that people will incrementally increase the number of new relationships as they move through the awareness and interest stages, and finally peak at the acceptance stage, where relationships are most critical to internalizing or adopting the ideology. The number of new relationships then declines as an individual remains in a cell and moves toward implementation despite continued cellular growth.

---

[45] Scott Helfstein, "Governance of Terror: New Institutionalism and the Evolution of Terrorist Organizations," *Public Administration Review* 69, no. 4 (July/August 2009), 727–739.
[46] McAdam (1986).

The second hypothesis pertains to the relationship between ideological affinity for extremism and social ties with like-minded individuals. Conventional wisdom would lead one to believe that there is an inverse relationship between these drivers of radical action whereby those with strong ideological affinity are more apt to accept the radical doctrine without many social ties. Individuals with weaker ideological affinity, by contrast, may require more social support to accept the doctrine. Ideological affinity in this sense reflects a personalogical characteristic of predisposition, which is integrated here with social dynamics. Testimonials from some disengaged radicals suggest that the violent views were actually quite shallow, and once people disengage from a social group there is little left to reinforce the extremist ideology.[47]

Figure 2: Social-Radicalization Predictions

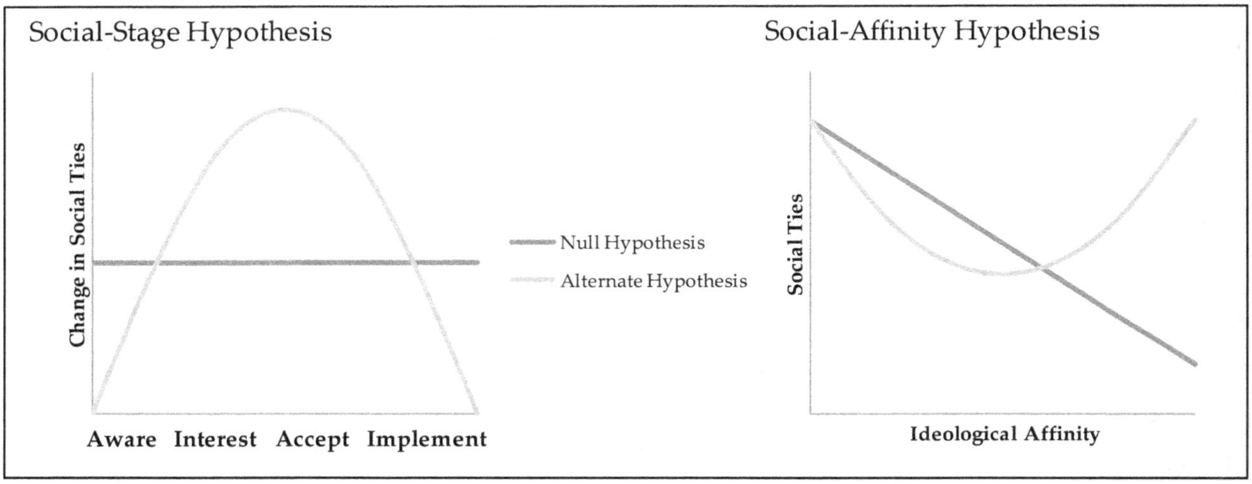

Al-Qa'ida's publicly available recruitment guide stresses targeting candidates with limited religious training or background, and then offers a strategy aimed at gradually deepening their social ties.[48] The most fruitful candidates would seem to be those susceptible to indoctrination through a process of socialization rather than religious training.[49] An extension of such logic would suggest that al-Qa'ida believes that those

---

[47] James Brandon, "The UK's Experience in Counter-Radicalization," *CTC Sentinel* 1, no. 5 (April 2008).

[48] Al-Qa'idi (2008).

[49] It is important to note that there is a difference between a prior, or someone's initial belief, and the conviction with which they hold that belief. The al-Qa'ida manual does not fully distinguish between these two aspects of belief, but they are of critical importance. Recruiting an individual who fully accepts the radical doctrine and has great conviction is relatively easy. By contrast, deeply religious individuals who reject the violent path, and hold that belief with great conviction, present a significant challenge that might not be worth the effort. The manual conflates these issues and both are important.

with weak affinity are best manipulated through social engagement. By contrast, Horgan's work on radicals in Northern Ireland challenges the "shallow" nature of ideology after disengagement.[50] Many of the subjects studied continued to profess strong ideological affinity for the cause after abandoning violence, and disengagement often seemed predicated on burnout or dissolution of social relationships. Horgan's work then gives reason to believe that the social relationships of those with strong ideological affinity may be as important to sustained engagement as it is for those with weak affinity.

On the one hand, al-Qa`ida's advice to adherents seems to support the idea that those with weak affinity are ideal candidates and that social relationships are crucial in recruiting such individuals. Should al-Qa`ida's instinct about the difficulty of recruiting those with stronger religious beliefs prove true, then social relationships could again prove critical to those on that side of the affinity spectrum as well. Together with Horgan's work, these insights challenge the notion that ideological affinity and social ties have an inverse relationship (the null hypothesis represented by the decreasing line on the graph in the right of Figure 2). Instead, social relationships may prove critical on both sides of the affinity spectrum. The Social-Affinity hypothesis, the alternate in Figure 2, offers a nonlinear prediction whereby social relationships are most important for those with weak affinity and decline in importance as affinity increases. Then this trend reverses, and social relationships again become more important as affinity strengthens.

This section has offered a conceptual framework for thinking about radicalization and the process that individuals move through on the way to violence. It subsequently showed how such a model can be used to develop hypotheses that counter conventional wisdom about radicalization and the role of social relationships in the process. The next section will focus on the tools used here to think about, capture and assess social relationships and changes over time.

---

[50] Horgan (2009).

The primary argument put forth here is that social process is central to radicalization, and that the importance of social relationships changes with the stages of radicalization and individual's personal characteristics. The purpose of this section is to assess the general relationship or importance of social interactions and radicalization before focusing on the specific hypothesis. In other words, what evidence is there that links radicalization and social interaction in the first place? How strong is the link, and when is it violated? Once these questions are assessed, the paper will apply some of the social network frameworks to unmask the nature—rather than just the importance—of social relationships in radical cells.

Hypothesis testing is one cornerstone of modern science, and it plays a prominent role for a simple reason: it allows one to consider all possible causal explanations and then exclude those that fail to receive empirical support.[51] Radicalization and social interaction are tightly coupled processes, and this analysis will challenge the idea that radicalization commonly occurs without social interaction. Once one has sufficient evidence to question the notion that people adopt radical ideologies in isolation, or without social interaction, it makes further study of social interaction critical.

The concept of the lone wolf terrorist offers an ideal window through which to examine this proposition. U.S. statutes technically associate a "lone wolf" with self-recruitment, two concepts that do not have clear definitional boundaries.[52] Terrorism analysts have often relied on the concept of the lone wolf to identify instances in which individuals choose to undertake violent action with political ends alone. It is important to provide a working definition here before moving forward. There is tendency to view lone wolves through the lens of execution, whereby individuals who perpetrate an attack by themselves are by definition lone wolves. Such a tactical emphasis proves a misleading course, since individuals like Richard Reid, the attempted shoe bomber, or Umar Farouk Abdulmutallab, the attempted Christmas Day bomber, who attempt to perpetrate violence by themselves but on behalf of groups, would be falsely labeled as

---

[51] In classical hypothesis testing, nothing is proven correct. Instead, knowledge is advanced by rejecting certain explanations. One devises a null and alternate hypothesis with the aim of disproving the null thereby validating the alternative. The importance of social interaction in radicalization will be assessed in an analogous fashion.

[52] Joshua Sinai, "How to Define Terrorism," *Perspectives on Terrorism* 2, no. 4 (2008).

lone wolves according to this definition.[53] In those two cases, individuals spent time preparing for the attacks with members with al-Qa`ida central and al-Qa`ida in the Arabian Peninsula, respectively.

Recognizing that the execution point does not offer a useful boundary, others turn to the planning phase, postulating that attacks planned and executed by individuals are lone wolf incidents.[54] By such a definition, Timothy McVeigh, the man responsible for the Oklahoma City Federal Building bomb, is a typical lone wolf. Such a definition presents similar difficulties. McVeigh planned and executed the attack on his own, but he had long history of engagement with radical right groups. On a tactical level, the attack was planned and executed by a single person, but that person had come to believe that the attack was justified, and even a moral imperative, through repeated interaction with a social community that validated and reinforced those beliefs. The radical ideology that guided his behavior in the planning and execution stages was already well established. In that sense, McVeigh was not a lone wolf, but a lone operating emissary with a long history of involvement with the radical right.

There are different ways one might define the lone wolf, distinguishing between mobilization, motivation and group identification. The mobilization definition emphasizes the lone operational context, discussed above, whereas a definition based on motivation might stress the development of unique radical doctrine. The definition put forth here incorporates all three, but stresses group identification. A lone wolf terrorist is an individual who plans or perpetrates an attack without a prior history of contact with social groups or organizations that operate with the aim of advancing shared radical political goals. The lone wolf comes to adopt a radical ideology on his or her own, without external influence, and then acts or attempts to act on those self-acquired beliefs. This is not to say that these people develop a unique ideological doctrine, but that they simply come to accept already existing doctrine without participating in any social contact. The key to identifying lone wolves, given this definition, is to have a clear picture of their social history and the method by which they came to act on a radical ideology. Such a definition makes lone wolf cases an ideal tool

---

[53] Raffaello Pantucci, "A Typology of Lone Wolves: Preliminary Analysis of Lone Islamist Terrorists," in *Developments in Radicalisation and Political Violence* (London, UK: International Centre for the Study of Radicalisation and Political Violence, 2011).

[54] Pantucci (2011) discusses different types of lone wolf attacks to orchestrate the difficulty to tying the definition to the attack itself.

to test the importance of social relationships and radicalization in the context of the current global militant jihadist threat.

Before looking at the relationship between radicalization and social interaction in more depth, it is worth looking across a series of attacks to assess whether social ties play a perceptible role in preparation and execution of terrorist acts. An assessment of eighty terrorist incidents both successful and failed during a seventeen-year period from 1993 to 2010 using the strict definition of a lone wolf attack developed above is instructive. Of the eighty attacks, forty-five were plotted, attempted or perpetrated by one person. This would make it seem as though the majority of these attacks were perpetrated by lone wolves, but this is the risk of overemphasizing a tactical definition. Many of these forty-five individuals in fact received training abroad or joined larger organizations at some point in their radicalization process. By looking at the social histories of individuals, there are approximately twenty instances of lone wolf attacks, comprising just over a quarter of the cases. It is also important to exclude a series of "platform" arrests, where law enforcement personnel make and develop social contacts with perpetrators given the definition of lone wolf advanced above.[55] In these instances, perpetrators attempt to develop social ties and reach out for assistance and validation. Given the legal guidelines and requirements in such investigations, these cases belie coding and do not fall simply into either category.

There are thirteen cases, shown in Table 1, of lone wolf terrorism employing the strict definition. Further investigation into each attack offers empirical reason to question the concept of lone wolf jihadist terrorism. Of the thirteen attacks, three were perpetrated by individuals drawing motivation from the Arab-Israeli conflict. The first lone wolf incident in the American jihad data set is the 1997 shootings at the Empire State Building by Ali Hassan Abu Kamal. Kamal was sixty-nine years of age and had been born in Jaffa, Palestine, and resettled to Gaza. Letters found after the attack blamed the United States, France and England for the plight of the Palestinians.[56] Hesham

---

[55] Terrorists arrested after making social contact with law enforcement agencies fall into an ambiguous category. Osman Mohamud, the young man who attempted to bomb the Christmas tree lighting in Portland, Oregon, in 2010, acted alone when he attempted to detonate the device. Before that culminating point, he believed that the undercover FBI agents who supplied him with a fake explosive device were al-Qa`ida members.

[56] N. R. Kleinfeld, "From Teacher to Gunman: U.S. Visit Ends in Fatal Rage," *New York Times* 25 February 1997.

Mohamed Hadayet, who opened fire at Los Angeles International Airport in 2002, targeted the El Al ticket counter. El Al is the official air carrier of Israel.[57] The third incident linked to the Arab-Israeli conflict is based on affinity for Hezbollah rather than the Palestinians. In 2007, Houssein Zorkot was arrested for carrying an AK-47 rifle through Hemlock Park in Dearborn, Michican, and the investigation subsequently revealed that he had recently traveled to Lebanon and posted messages on a Hezbollah chat board.[58] Al-Qa`ida's global jihadist ideology often invokes the Arab-Israeli conflict as justification for joining its ranks.[59]

Table 1: Lone Wolves in American Jihad

Year	Perpetrator	Location	Israel Palestine/ Hezbollah	Personal Mental Health/ Counterculture	Never Committed Violence
1997	Kamal	New York, NY	Yes		
2002	Bishop	Tampa, FL		Yes	
2002	Hadayet	Los Angeles, CA	Yes		
2003	Akbar	Kuwait		Yes	
2004	Anderson	Tacoma, WA			Yes
2005	Shah	Beacon, NY			Yes
2006	Taheri-Azar	Chapel Hill, NC		Yes	
2006	Haq	Seattle, WA		Yes	
2007	Talović	Salt Lake City, UT		Yes	
2007	Abujihaad	Phoenix, AZ			Yes
2007	Zorkot	Dearborn, MI	Yes		
2007	Ahmad	Homestead AFB		Yes	
2009	Hassan	Fort Hood, TX			

Individual circumstances, either mental stability or alienation, played a key role in the escalation to violence in six of the thirteen cases. Following the model of the September 11 attacks, the fifteen-year-old Charles Bishop crashed a Cessna 172 plane into a Tampa, Florida, office building in 2002. Officials believed the crash was a suicide attempt despite finding a letter that voiced support for Osama bin Laden, but a subsequent

[57] Charles Feldman, "Federal Investigators: L.A. Airport Shooting a Terrorist Act," *CNN Los Angeles Bureau* 4 September 2002, accessed online 3 August 2011.

[58] Sean Delaney, "Man With AK-47 Assault Rifle Arrested After Leaving Dearborn's Hemlock Park," *Free Press* 12 September 2007, accessed online 3 August 2011.

[59] Robert Wesley, "Understanding Al-Qa'ida's Grievance Framing," in *Making the Grade: Assessing al-Qa'ida's Learning and Adaptation*, ed. Scott Helfstein (West Point, NY: Combating Terrorism Center, 2009).

discovery surrounding a lawsuit over an acne medicine made by Hoffman-La Roche laboratories revealed a family history with depression and suicidal tendencies.[60] In 2006, Naveed Afzal Haq opened fire at the Jewish Federation of Greater Seattle. While the jury rejected the argument that Haq was criminally insane, he had a history mental problems and counterculture behavior. Reports suggest that Haq was bipolar, taking medication for the disorder, and had previous brushes with the law, including public exposure and a series of traffic violations.[61] He also renounced Islam and was baptized in 2005, but seemed depressed by the familial conflict that ensued after his conversion.[62] Tahmeed Ahmad's attack on Homestead AFB in Florida with knives and vodka bottles also involved an individual with a history of psychological problems. Ahmad's mother reported that he had recently been in a mental institution.[63] The history of psychological problems across these individuals does not mean that a radical jihadist ideology was irrelevant. Quite the contrary, the ideology may have provided critical validation for these people to act. In these cases, however, the absence of social relationships with others who have also adopted this radical ideology was also accompanied by mental issues.

Three other cases offer examples of individuals who either found themselves isolated from their peers or chose to isolate themselves. Sulejman Talović opened fire in Salt Lake City's Trolley Square mall. He was born in the Vlasenica municipality of Bosnia and Herzegovina and lived through the ethnic cleansing of the 1990s. Reports show that he had few friends, some minor juvenile offenses and had dropped out of school at sixteen.[64] Mohammed Reza Taheri-azar, the driver who attempted to kill a number of people with his car in Chapel Hill, North Carolina, adopted a series of unusual behaviors and found himself isolated from peers. Taheri-azar later reported that he was trying to follow in the footsteps of Mohammad Atta, one of the September 11 hijackers, suggesting that there is a clear connection to global jihad. At the same time, he had a

---

[60] Carrie Weimar, "Teen Pilot's Family Drops Drug Lawsuit: The 15-Year-Old Killed Himself by Crashing a Plane into a High-Rise," *St. Petersburg Times* 28 June 2007, accessed online 3 August 2011.

[61] Tracy Johnson, "Murder Charge in Shootings at Jewish Federation: Prosecutor Could Seek the Death Penalty for Haq," *Seattle P-I* 2 August 2006, accessed online 3 August 2011; "Incidents Clash with Image Suspect Conveyed in School," *Seattle Times* 30 July 2006, accessed online 3 August 2011.

[62] The social dynamics of renouncing religion or traditions is worthy of further attention. There are often aspects of shame and manipulation that may prove powerful motivational tools.

[63] "FBI: Teacher who Attacked MPs was Suicidal," *Associated Press* 23 October 2007, accessed online 3 August 2011.

[64] "Police: Off-Duty Cop Saved Lives In Mall," *CNSNews* 11 February 2009, accessed August 3, 2011.

history of counterculture behavior, from serious traffic violations to awkward religious practices.[65] The third case involves Hasan Karim Akbar, the perpetrator of a grenade-and-shooting attack at Camp Pennsylvania, Kuwait. His lawyers claimed that he had a history of mental illness, and he appears to have had strong reservations about his involvement in the army preceding the invasion of Iraq. There is some evidence to suggest that he acted as a response to mistreatment by fellow soldiers who isolated and berated him, but there is little in his behavior to suggest that he adopted al-Qa'ida's globalist ideology.[66]

Three of the thirteen cases in Table 1 involve individuals caught in the process of reaching out to develop social connections before actually committing violence. This represents an interesting challenge, since it is difficult to determine the degree of radicalization prior to the social contact. It is interesting that all of them reached out to others prior to taking a violent act, perhaps in the hope of acquiring capabilities, gaining bona fides or obtaining validation. While it is impossible to eliminate any of the likely explanations with certainty, the cases seem to reflect individuals at the entry stages of jihad trying to build good faith and social ties with militants. Two of these cases involved U.S. military personnel who offered sensitive information online. Ryan Anderson, a specialist in the 81st Armored Brigade of the Army National Guard, was arrested in 2004. The FBI had monitored his online activity on al-Qa'ida chat rooms, and he subsequently offered tactical information to undercover agents.[67] Anderson's lawyers argued that he had history of bipolar disorder and that he used online role-playing games to structure his social interactions. Subsequently, naval enlisted Paul Hall, also known as Hassan Abu-Jihaad, was arrested in 2007 for disclosing sensitive information on ship movements.[68] He later admitted to sympathizing with the enemy. The third case is that of Tarik Shah, convicted of offering support to al-Qa'ida in 2005. Shah was a New York musician with training in the martial arts who was arrested by

---

[65] Stancill and Rocha (2006).

[66] Shaila Dewan, "Trial Opens for Sergeant Accused of Killing 2 Officers," *New York Times* 12 April 2005, accessed online 3 August 2011.

[67] Eli Sanders, "Guardsman Given Life in Prison for Trying to Help Al Qaeda," *New York Times* 4 September 2004 accessed online 4 August 2011.

[68] Josh White, "Former Sailor Accused of Providing Data to Terrorist Web Site," *Washington Post* 8 March 2007, accessed online 4 August 2011.

undercover agents when he volunteered to train al-Qa'ida in Iraq fighters.[69] All of these cases involved individuals trying to connect with radical elements either online or in person, but none of them crossed the threshold of committing violent acts themselves.

The final case in the table is that of Nidal Hassan, the Foot Hood shooter. The Hassan case is difficult to categorize, in part because some of the information on his social interaction remains classified. Hassan appears to be a prototypical lone wolf who radicalized on his own and then perpetrated an act of violence. The complicating factor is that in the process of adopting his radical beliefs, Hassan reached out on multiple occasions to the radical cleric Anwar al-Awlaki, a member of al-Qa'ida in the Arabian Peninsula who was killed in a missile strike.[70] This reflects two parallel processes. The first typifies self-radicalization, whereby Hassan gradually deepened his commitment to the ideology over time. The second reflects his desire for social ties and external validation as he proceeded down the path. Even if one views Nidal Hassan's attack as a case of lone wolf jihadist terrorism, it remains an outlier.

Across the subset of lone wolf cases in the universe of plots, it is hard to find strong evidence of perpetrators' adopting radical beliefs, and specifically al-Qa'ida's brand of global jihadist militancy. It might seem that the argument here rejects the possibility of lone wolf jihadism, but this is not the case. Lone wolf attacks can happen and continue to pose a threat, particularly as the online landscape evolves and it becomes easier for people to encounter radical ideological discourse. Historical analysis of attack casualties also offers reason for concern, as the predicted relationship between perpetrators and casualties shown in Figure 3 shows that lone wolf attacks tend to be as deadly as those with twenty-five perpetrators. (This assessment relied on the Global Terrorism Database and included incidents where the number of perpetrators was known and less than twenty-five.[71]) Rather than reject or downplay the risks posed by lone wolves, the argument here is that individuals perpetrating lone wolf attacks on behalf of the global jihadist movement remain an exception rather than the rule.

---

[69] Alan Feuer, "Bronx Man Pleads Guilty In Terror Case," *New York Times* 5 April 2007, accessed online 28 July 2011.

[70] David Johnston and Scott Shane, "U.S. Knew of Suspect's Tie to Radical Cleric," *New York Times* 9 November 2009, accessed online 4 August 2011.

[71] National Consortium for the Study of Terrorism and Responses to Terrorism (START) (2011), Global Terrorism Database, retrieved from http://www.start.umd.edu/gtd.

Only thirteen of eighty cases met the definition of lone wolf terrorism advanced here, and of those, twelve of the cases involved individuals motivated by the Arab-Israeli conflict, deep-seated personal issues or social validation as they became more radical. With the possible exception of Nidal Hassan, the only lone wolf cases exhibiting a clear commitment to al-Qa'ida's notion of global jihad were individuals in the early stages seeking validation. Even Taheri-azar, who both pursued his doctorate and attacked in emulation of Mohammad Atta, failed to act in ways that reflect his acceptance or adoption of al-Qa'ida's religious doctrine. The logical conclusion is that social ties play a central role in the adoption of extremist beliefs or norms, and there is good reason to explore how such relationships affect the trajectory of violent cells. The plurality of terrorist cases assessed here are not classified as lone wolf incidents according the definition developed above, meaning that social interactions play an important role in this evolving threat and there is an important need to better understand how and why those dynamics matter.

Figure 3: Average Casualties by Perpetrators

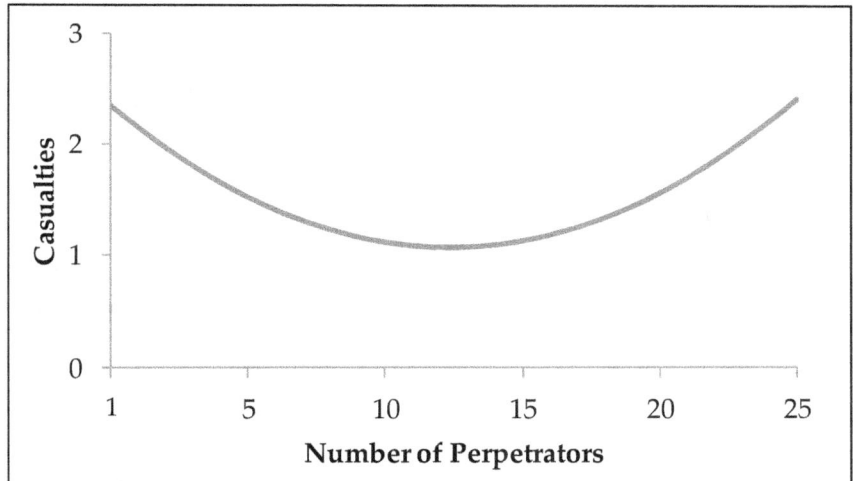

Note: Analysis relied on negative binomial regression model with causalities as the dependent variable excluding attacks with missing data and more than 25 perpetrators. The regression results are presented as Variable Coefficient (Standard Errors, p-Value): Perpetrators −0.20 (0.01, p<0.01), Perpetrators^2 0.01 (0.00, P<0.01), and Constant 2.36 (0.03, p<0.01).

The next section looks at the role of social relationships in terrorist plots, specifically as it relates to radicalization, and then applies some basic tools to identify the strengths and weaknesses of terrorist social networks. After taking a snapshot of key social characteristics of some cells, the social network paradigm is leveraged to assess the radicalization hypotheses developed above.

The network paradigm is increasingly common in different spheres ranging across the scientific, policy and tactical communities. This is particularly true for analyses of terrorism, where the network paradigm seems a natural way to talk about groups with fluid borders that often defy conventional paradigms and taxonomies. At their core, terrorist and insurgents groups are made up of individuals who share social connections to one another, which is definition of a social network. This simple definition, however, masks some of the nuances of networks and the role they play in affecting outcomes. For example, different network structures, or arrangements of ties across individuals, may convey very different advantages and disadvantages.[72] Not all networks are created equal. For the purpose of this project, the edges, the term that network scientists use for the relationships that tie different individuals, are particularly important. It is the edges that provide the pathways through which radical ideas can flow between individuals and that cells use to facilitate operational planning, mobilization and conduct of terrorist operations. In the study of radicalization, and especially the social dynamics of radicalization, the evolution of network structure and node-edge relationships offer an avenue for valuable insights.

Network analysis examines how different arrangements of node-edge structures evolve and how networks might affect either the behavior of things in the network or the surrounding environment outside. The network paradigm can be applied in many ways, such as a highway system where cities are nodes and the roads connecting them edges; in ecology where nodes are different species and edges reflect predator-prey relationship; or biology where proteins are nodes and their interactions are represented by edges. In social networks, nodes usually represent people and the connections or social ties between them are characterized by edges that link them together. Figure 4 shows a sample social network, highlighting three concepts: node, edge, and giant component. The giant component, which will be examined later in more detail, simply refers to the largest group of connected individuals. This offers a simple yet powerful method to assess social dynamics and group evolution.

---

[72] Candace Jones, William S. Hesterly and Stephen P. Borgatti, "A General Theory of Network Governance," *Academy of Management Review* 22, no. 4 (1997), 911–46; Joel M. Podolny and Karen L. Page, "Network Forms of Organization," *Annual Review of Sociology* 24 (1998), 57–76; and Mette Eilstrup-Sangiovanni and Calvert Jones, "Assessing the Dangers of Illicit Networks: Why al-Qaida May Be Less Threatening Than Many Think," *International Security* 33, no. 2 (2008), 7–44.

Figure 4: Social Networks

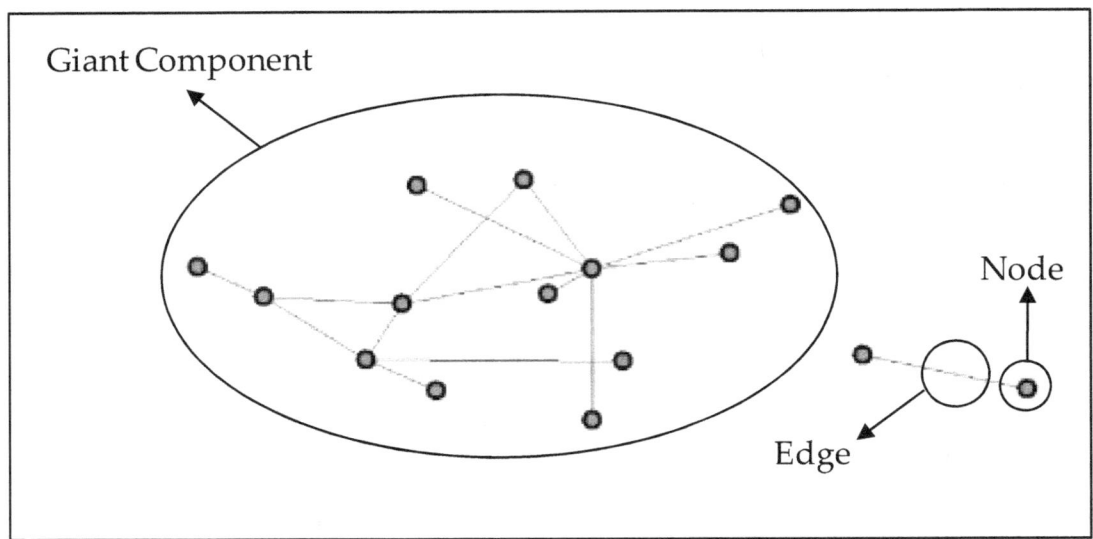

This project will draw on four common measures of network features in exploring the social processes of radicalization. The measure of centrality offers different ways of thinking about behavior, social roles and power in networks. Centrality refers to the primacy of the node or individual, and there are different ways to think about centrality in networks. Each measure will first be explored independently, and then they will be paired to develop some useful analytical structures for characterizing behavior and capabilities. The discussion below will not offer a detailed mathematical exposition of each measure, which can be found elsewhere, but instead aims to provide descriptions of each along with some intuition behind the mathematical characteristics.[73]

The most common and simple network measure employed is referred to as degree centrality. Degree simply counts the number of connections that a node or individual has with others. This is a simple summation for each node in the network. Often there are underlying patterns that emerge in the study of networks, particularly in measures of degree centrality. For example, many networks display power law distribution whereby many nodes have very few connections and a few nodes have many connections. One shorthand for this principle is referred to as the 80-20 Rule where 20

---

[73] For mathematical derivations see Mark Newman, *Networks: An Introduction* (Oxford, UK: Oxford University Press, 2010); and David Knoke and Song Yang, "Social Network Analysis," Sage University Paper Series on Quantitative Applications in the Social Sciences, no. 154 (London, UK: Sage Publications, 2007).

percent of the people have 80 percent of the connections.[74] There is nothing hard and fast about 80-20 per se, and networks display variance in connectivity, but many large networks such as the Internet and metabolic systems were found to have power law distributions in degree centrality that approximate 80-20. Interestingly, work on terrorist cells has proved to challenge such a rule as ties are more evenly distributed throughout the membership.[75] There are strengths and weaknesses of degree as a measure of centrality. The greatest advantage lies in its simplicity, but that is also where it can be misleading. It would seem that more connections are better than few, but many such connections may tie to nodes that are relatively unimportant. It is also a fairly simple and possibly deceptive indicator of one's position in the network relative to others. Degree centrality will be used sparingly, and for very specific purposes, for these reasons in the analysis that follows.

A second common measure in network studies is eigenvector centrality. While having the disadvantage of being more complicated than degree centrality it offers some modest improvements in detailing individual network profiles. Eigenvector centrality measures the quality of one's connections based on the number of connections that fiends have. In other words, it expresses how many well-connected individuals one links with. The measure assigns a higher value to nodes whose connections have a relatively large number of links versus nodes with the same number of connections that have fewer links themselves.[76] By asking how many well-connected individuals any node is tied to, eigenvector centrality offers a way of thinking about connections beyond one's immediate neighbors.

Betweenness centrality is another useful measure for describing the role of an individual or node that looks at an individual's ability to link disparate parts of a network. In short, it captures whether a node lies on the path between any other two nodes. Those with high betweenness are typically thought of as boundary spanners, or individuals part of many different communities or cliques. These people help to connect

---

[74] Albert-Laszlo Barabási, *Linked: How Everything Is Connected to Everything Else and What It Means* (New York, NY: Plume Books, 2003).

[75] Scott Helfstein and Dominick Wright (2011).

[76] For detailed discussions on eigenvector centrality see Rosanna Grassi, Silvana Stefani and Ann Torriero, "Some New Results on the Eigenvector Centrality," *Journal of Mathematical Sociology* 31, no. 3 (2007), 237–248; and Phillip Bonacich, "Some Unique Properties of Eigenvector Centrality," *Social Networks* 29, no. 4 (October 2007), 555–564.

subgroups that might otherwise never interact. Since no other member of a subgroup can interact with members of the other without the boundary spanner, interactions between these groups rely on that common node. This is an extreme example where there might only be one common link between subgroups, but it proves useful in explaining how individuals with such characteristics might play a unique role in networks. Betweenness centrality is calculated by summing the number of times that a node is found on the shortest path between any two other nodes relative to the total number of shortest paths between those nodes.[77] By focusing on individuals that lie along these shortest paths, betweenness becomes an excellent way to think about access points and connectivity among groups.

The final centrality measure employed in this analysis is closeness, which literally looks at how close one node is to others. In this sense, close is not defined geographically, but through relationships in the network. Those that have high closeness can travel very short distances through the network and still reach a large number of people, which is to say that they are firmly embedded in many subgroups or cliques. It improves on degree centrality by incorporating those nodes beyond immediate reach, or the first degree. The individual with high betweenness transverses subgroups, but might not maintain close relations with more than a few members. Individuals with high closeness tend to be embedded in such groups and can access many people within subgroups with relatively little effort. Those with high closeness centrality are well positioned to monitor behavior and flows in the network, because they have relatively short paths to others. Such nodes are well suited to functions like monitoring or facilitation given their accessibility to others. Closeness is calculated by taking the average of the shortest distance, or path length, between one node and all others in the network measured by how many edges must be traveled through.[78]

Each of these measures individually elucidates something about the nodes in a network. Degree centrality captures the number of relationships. Eigenvector centrality shows how connected people are to well-connected individuals. Betweenness offers a way to

[77] Linton C. Freeman, "A Set of Measures of Centrality Based on Betweenness," *Sociometry* 40, no. 1 (March 1977), 35–41.
[78] Timothy J. Rowley, "Moving beyond Dyadic Ties: A Network Theory of Stakeholder Influences," *Academy of Management Review* 22, no. 4 (October 1997), 887–910.

think about boundary spanning or bridging among groups. Finally, closeness captures the ease with which people can access others.

The radicalization framework proposed earlier outlined four stages through which an ideal recruit passes: awareness, interest, acceptance and implementation. Given prior work on high-risk social activism and a review of radicalization literature, two hypotheses were developed that explicitly linked radicalization and social interaction. The first hypotheses, directly tied to the framework, argued that the importance of social ties changes as people move through the different stages. A second argument then addressed the relationship between an individual's ideological affinity and his or her social ties. These arguments are tested below, and then the taxonomies are extended to further explicate the relationship of social ties, radicalization and network structure.

The social network data, with modest manipulation, can offer insight into the two hypotheses developed above. The Social-Stage hypothesis suggests that the importance of social relationships changes as people move through the different stages of radicalization. In the awareness, social dynamics should prove least important. An individual may come to encounter a radical ideology through a social tie, but it is just as easy for initial exposure to occur through the media or the Internet. Social ties become more important in the interest stage as aware individuals determine whether they want to proceed further down the path of radicalization. Social relationships help entice those interested in identity or status seeking in particular, but may also play a role for those with other motivations as well. Social interaction is most vital at the acceptance stage, where external validation is critical to the adoption of a radical norm or belief set. Once people come to internalize these ideas, the social relationships become marginally less important with the movement to the implementation stage. This is not say that social ties become irrelevant in implementation, and in fact, social relationships are often important to sustaining involvement once an individual has become radicalized. Instead, the argument here is that it becomes less critical to seek external validation at this stage.

The network data can show patterns of social interaction over time, critical to testing this hypothesis. The nonlinear importance of social relationships is analogous to an increasing desire to form new social ties with radical individuals as one begins exploring a radical ideology, ultimately culminating at the acceptance stage. Individuals who progress beyond that stage should have less incentive and interest in forming further relationships. The tendency to form new relationships involves calculating the change in degree centrality from one period to the next. Degree is a measure of centrality that simply counts the number of ties with other individuals. It is fairly straightforward to interpret changes in degree, since it is not weighted, as the number of new relationships from one period to the next. A positive number implies that individuals added ties and negative number means they severed or lost ties during the period. Change in degree, therefore, offers a way to capture and illustrate the trajectory of social interaction as people move through the radicalization process.

The Social-Stage hypothesis is evaluated using the change in degree and the time that people were connected to the giant component. In network parlance, the giant component represents the largest group of connected individuals. The giant component is the group of people that ultimately commits the attack in the data considered here. Early in the life of a terror cell, there is some small group that constitutes the beginnings of the giant component. Over time, people drift into the giant component orbit, perhaps individually or with some prior social relationships, and then connect to someone who brings them into the would-be cell. The question then, is whether a discernable pattern emerges in relationship formation over time once people are exposed to a radical social group. The Social-Stage hypothesis predicts that such a pattern should be evident and that the change in degree along with time in the giant component can be used to assess whether it empirically exists in this data.

The analysis of the John Jay and Artis data shows that the Social-Stage hypothesis receives strong confirmation.[79] Individuals gradually increase the number of new relationships they make once they have been linked to the giant component for a period of time, but then the tendency to form new relationships decreases despite continued cellular growth. Figure 5 shows the predicted pattern of new link formation over time. When individuals form their first tie to a radical group, there is a tendency to form subsequent relationships with other group members. Statistical analysis shows that the predicted number of new relationships per period, approximately one year, increases to a maximum of two and half just beyond the halfway point in cell longevity. Once reaching the maximum, the predicted number of new links per period declines rapidly despite the fact that the cells continue to add new members in an approximately linear

---

[79] Scott Helfstein and Dominick Wright (2011).

fashion until the attack. New entrants into these radical groups have tendency to increase the contact with fellow participants, just as the hypothesis predicts. The importance of social interaction can also be examined through a sensitivity analysis that reflects statistical differences in the tendency to form new relationships, where there is a greater tendency to generate new ties early on and new ties are less prominent once an individual has spent time in the network. These analyses suggest that the search for external validation increases and then decreases as people progress through the stages of radicalization.

Figure 5: Statistical Estimation of Social Relationships

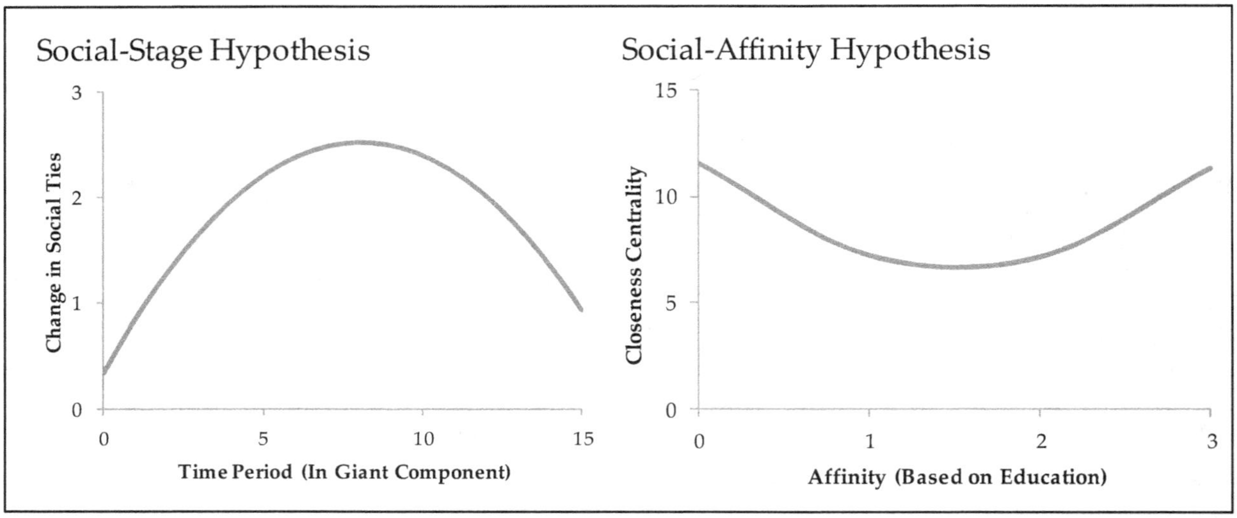

Note: Analysis relied on linear regression model and results are robust to fixed and random effects specification. The Social-Stage dependent variable is change in social ties. The regression results are presented as Variable Coefficient (Standard Errors, p-Value): Time in Giant Component 0.54 (0.05, $p<0.01$), Time in Giant Component^2 −0.03 (0.00, $p<0.01$), Time Period Control −0.11 (0.01, $p<0.01$), and Constant 1.76 (0.21, $p<0.01$). The Social-Affinity dependent variable is closeness. The regression results are presented as Variable Coefficient (Standard Errors, p-Value): Education Type −6.55 (2.37, $p<0.01$), Education Type^2 2.15 (0.80, $p<0.01$), and Constant 11.61 (1.73, $p<0.01$).

The nonlinear trajectory of relationship formation and the differential effects of social relationships in different stages have some serious implications for disrupting the process of radicalization. The individuals in the lone wolf cases who were arrested before attempting to execute violent acts were all caught in the process of seeking social ties and external validation, whether online or through personal contact. People who progress through the stages in a more or less linear form become most susceptible to intervention as the need for external validation and social ties increases in the

44

acceptance stage for two reasons. First, the need to form social relationships means that these individuals are seeking out and open to approach in the virtual or the real world. Opportunities exist to alter the makeup of the new relationships they form. Second, they are also vulnerable because acceptance is the most difficult stage to progress through without social support, meaning that individuals at this point may be emotionally or ideologically volatile. Those purporting radical ideas and seeking to recruit individuals in person or through mass propaganda rely on this emotional vulnerability to achieve the cognitive liberation needed for individuals to reject their old beliefs and adopt the new one. This same vulnerability window offers an equally important opportunity to intervene if performed with care to avoid reaffirming the radical position.

The second hypothesis, Social-Affinity, suggests that the relationship between social ties and ideological affinity among radicals may display some nonlinear patterns as well. Conventional wisdom would argue that individuals with ideological affinity, because of upbringing or personal beliefs, should need less social support to accept a radical ideology and justify involvement. By contrast, Mark Tessler's research shows that religiosity is a poor predictor of support for al-Qa`ida and terrorism in the Middle East, and Horgan shows that people with strong ideological affinity can disengage from violence by changing their social network.[80] This offers reason to revisit the Social-Affinity relationship, because those with an ideological predisposition may find social ties to those with little ideological affinity equally as important as those to other like-minded individuals. This proposition can be explored with social network analysis.

The measure of ideological affinity used to test this hypothesis was school experience. Individuals were coded to reflect the type of school they attended. Those who attended a secular school were coded zero, a religious (not necessarily Islamic) school received a one, a madrassa coded two, and a radical madrassa coded three. The education data were gathered as part of the John Jay data set, and the coding was modified for this analysis to reflect an increasing ideological predisposition toward radical militant Islam. Thus, those with higher scores on education type received more exposure to religious ideas in their formative experience, possibly translating to a greater ideological affinity for radical doctrine supporting violent action irrespective of social ties.

---

[80] Mark Tessler, "Arab and Muslim Political Attitudes: Stereotypes and Evidence from Survey Research," *International Studies Perspectives* 4, no. 2 (May 2003), 175–181; Horgan (2009).

Testing the Social-Affinity hypothesis pairs the education variable with closeness centrality. Closeness provides an ideal measure of social bonds by looking at how tightly an individual is tied with those around him or her, which offers some conceptual advantages relative to other measures. Degree captures the number of social ties, but it does not offer insight into the interconnection of those relationships beyond the single actor to gain a sense of cohesion. Similarly, eigenvector centrality weights relationships by looking at the connections of those tied to the individual, but lacks a measurement of interconnectedness. Betweenness presents similar issues, focusing instead on the role of people in linking disparate social groups rather than the depth of their relationships to people within those groups. By looking at the pathways through the network, and individual access to short paths, closeness offers a measure of social connectivity that integrates both relationships and interpersonal cohesion within the social group. The measure of closeness is taken at the period of initial entry into the giant component. It is this formative stage where the predicted effects of the Social-Affinity hypothesis should prove most important in the radicalization process.

Analysis reveals that the relationship between ideological affinity and social ties does not follow a simple inverse relationship. Instead, it displays a more complicated nonlinear pattern. Figure 5 shows the predicted relationship between ideological affinity on the horizontal axis and social relationships measured by closeness on the vertical axis. Just as the Social-Affinity hypothesis predicts, those with low affinity have fairly high measures of social connectivity. The connectivity decreases as affinity increases, initially following an inverse trajectory, but subsequently reverses. Social connectivity then increases as ideological affinity increases, confirming the alternate hypothesis that social interaction may prove just as important for those with high affinity as it does for those with low affinity. In fact, the predicted closeness scores for those with the lowest and highest affinity scores are almost identical. The statistical analysis predicts great symmetry at the extremes of the scale. In short, social relationships appear to play an equally important role for those with low and high affinity as people radicalize and join extremist cells.

The strong empirical evidence of the two primary hypotheses advanced here suggests that social interaction is far more integrated in the basic fabric of radicalization than often acknowledged in studies of extremist behavior. There are systemic relationships between social ties, the process and the predisposition to participate in terrorist activity.

These hypotheses just scratch the surface but suggest that there are many lessons nestled between the social, behavioral and ideological dimensions of the problem.

There is ample evidence that social relationships prove a critical factor in radicalization, and perhaps more important, there are general patterns in the development of those ties. The edges that bind people in social networks help to ensure that radical ideology is passed among members and that extremist norms are then reinforced and validated. Social relationships are important at the entry level, but are critical in the intermediate periods of radicalization and involvement. Disrupting the formation and utilization of these ties offers one method of short-circuiting the radicalization process. This course will not prevent individuals from seeking out radical doctrine, but it may prove critical to diverting their interests elsewhere.

Recall that four approaches for evaluating network position were described above: degree centrality, eigenvector centrality, betweenness and closeness. Each of these measures individually elucidates something about the nodes in a network.

These measures can also be aggregated to help characterize how nodes or individuals might function in a social network. There are two such taxonomies offered here. These taxonomies are discussed in the context of social networks and applied to radicalization as the topic at hand, but they are sufficiently general that they could apply to any networks of interest. One is focused on the properties of nodes populating the network and the other emphasizes the pathways or edges through the network. Mapping networks on these taxonomies can help identify the types of functional strengths and weaknesses of different systems or structures.

The first taxonomy, shown in Figure 6, integrates eigenvector and betweenness centralities to identify the characteristics and functions of individuals in the network. The Node Taxonomy illustrates how an individual's role might change as he or she varies across the two centrality measures. Those with higher eigenvector centrality scores, actors connected to the well-connected, are often thought of as gatekeepers. Nodes with high betweenness, the boundary spanners, are often thought of as brokers or mediators.[81] When individuals have low scores on both measures and lie near the axis in the lower left quadrant, they are considered peripheral players. One interpretation of these individuals is that they lack importance and play little role in network function.[82] In that case, these people may play a critical role in bringing in resources or information from outside. Those with high closeness scores and relatively lower eigenvector scores, the upper left quadrant, are prototypical gatekeepers. By contrast, individuals in the lower right quadrant with high betweenness and low eigenvector score are brokers. Those who score high in both categories, super brokers, tie to well-connected individuals across different communities.

---

[81] Valdis Krebs, "Social Network Analysis, A Brief Introduction," orgnet.com, accessed online 21 August 2011.

[82] Another interpretation of peripheral players is that these people may lack centrality in the network under study, but connect it to networks not represented in the graph.

The characterization of a network across these two spectrums helps to anticipate its structural and functional capacities. For example, networks endowed with a great deal of individuals with high betweenness might display greater innovative capacities, since brokers and boundary spanners can carry ideas between subgroups. Those with greater numbers of gatekeepers might be more geared to analytical and deliberative action, since the well-connected individuals can correspond with a number of individuals rather than an insular advising cadre.

Figure 6: Network Taxonomies

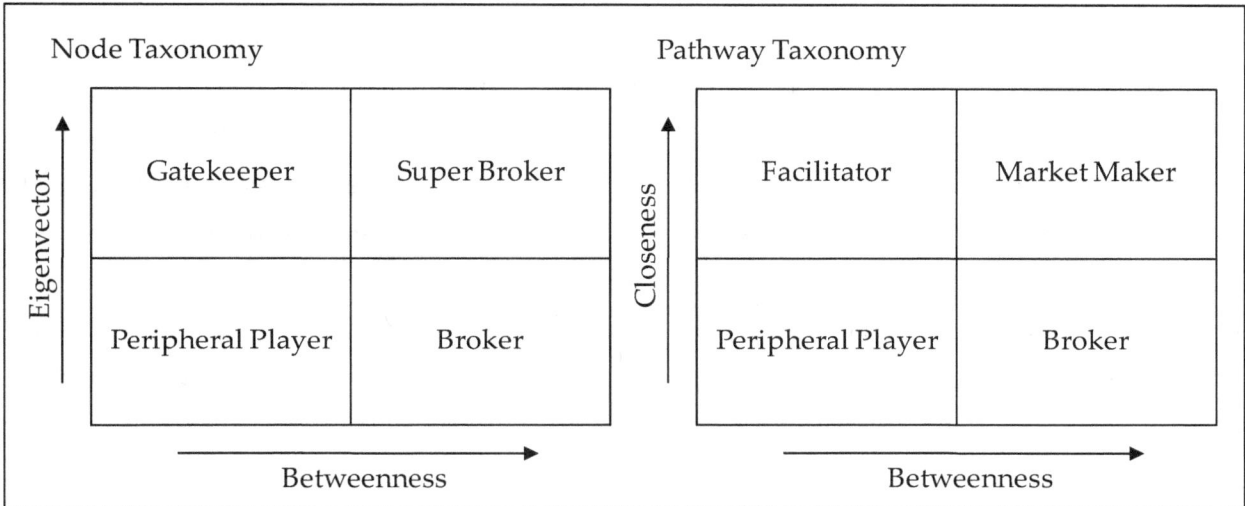

The Pathway Taxonomy, the second categorization shown in Figure 6, offers insight into how resources such as information may move through networks and how efficient networks may be in managing flows. Similar to the taxonomy above, betweenness lies on the horizontal axis. Betweenness, in the first taxonomy, plays a key role in understanding how well people can bridge between groups. The emphasis here is on the network's ability to move things through pathways. Networks lacking high betweenness nodes will find that resources tend to accrue in subsections of the network with little capacity to distribute or deploy to other parts even if such a change would offer a more efficient utilization. They simply lack the pathways relative to networks with nodes that have more brokers. Closeness is also a valuable way to think about the movement of resources through the network, since it actually averages the number of edges or length of pathways between people. Individuals who can access others with little effort can facilitate interaction, transfer material and monitor behavior. Since the pathway taxonomy is transaction oriented, nodes with lower betweenness and closeness scores are merely supporting elements with limited capacity to improve efficiency. Those with higher levels of closeness in the upper left quadrant play a facilitation role, and those with higher betweenness in the lower right continue to play the broker or spanner role. Those with higher closeness and betweenness scores are market makers, people capable of facilitating transactions between diverse groups through multiple channels with little difficulty.

Networks populated by individuals with high levels of betweenness and low levels of closeness find it easy to move resources between subgroups, but find it difficult to channel those resources through the clique. By contrast, those with high closeness should be able to facilitate action within the subgroup, but will find it difficult to move material or ideas between subgroups. Tasks better suited to small isolated teams will prove easier for networks with high closeness and lower betweenness. As the importance of coordination between close-knit teams increases, betweenness becomes more important. Research shows that decentralized teams are better at solving simple tasks, but more complicated tasks often require some degree of central coordination.[83] Thus, the distribution of node characteristics across these two measures can be instructive.

The basic tools discussed here offer a powerful way to characterize social relationships. These are not the only tools available, and social network theory is only one of many ways to assess the behavior of social groups, but there has been little application in systemic fashion to the pressing problem of radicalization. In part, this may stem from the belief that radicalization is inherently an internal, psychological process and social networks capture extroverted rather than introverted activity. To the extent that radicalization takes place in isolation of social ties, this argument would undoubtedly find support. The arguments put forth here suggest that radicalization and social relationships are often inseparable, and it is important to assess the interaction of ideas and relationships to gain a richer understanding of this complex process. While the social network approach may swing the pendulum too far from the introspective, ideological approach, it will hopefully help offer a step towards bridging the two.

---

[83] Ken Kollman, John H. Miller and Scott E. Page (2000).

Given the importance of social relationships in belief or norm adoption evidenced in the lone wolf cases, social network analysis offers one method of assessing intragroup relationships to better understand radicalization. Unfortunately, such studies require data on the evolution of group ties, which is to say networks that show change over time, and there are few sources available for such analysis. In fact, the rigorous study of terrorist organizations and cells has been hindered by limited data availability and the high costs of collecting new data. The one open source data set that shows changes in the network over time, often referred to as longitudinal data, comes from the John Jay and Artis project.[84] The data set shows the evolution of six terrorist cells, five from Southeast Asia and the Madrid train bombing cell. While much of the data comes from Southeast Asia, the Madrid cell acts as an out-of-sample comparison to assess whether the findings generalize beyond a specific geographic context.[85] The data offer a unique opportunity to assess terror networks and how social structure and radicalization interact.

Before evaluating the hypothesis specifically linking radicalization to social relationships developed above, the rest of this section will apply the social network taxonomies across the attacks as a snapshot of their social structure. Figure 7 shows the Node and Pathway Taxonomies for each of the six cells in the period where the attack was perpetrated, and there are some common emergent patterns that should help shape shared understanding of these violent social networks. Beginning with the Node Taxonomies, where betweenness is placed on the horizontal axis and eigenvector centrality on the vertical axis, the six attacks show a very modest relationship between higher levels of betweenness and higher eigenvector scores. This implies that people acting as boundary spanners who link different subgroups exhibit a modest tendency to connect to well-connected individuals.

---

[84] See http://www.jjay.cuny.edu/centers/terrorism/ and http://sandbox.artisresearch.com/.

[85] The five attacks from Southeast Asia are spread over time and include the first and second Bali Bombings, the Christmas Eve attack, the attack on the Philippine Ambassador's residence, and the Australian Embassy attack spanning five years.

Figure 7: Cells in Node and Pathway Taxonomies

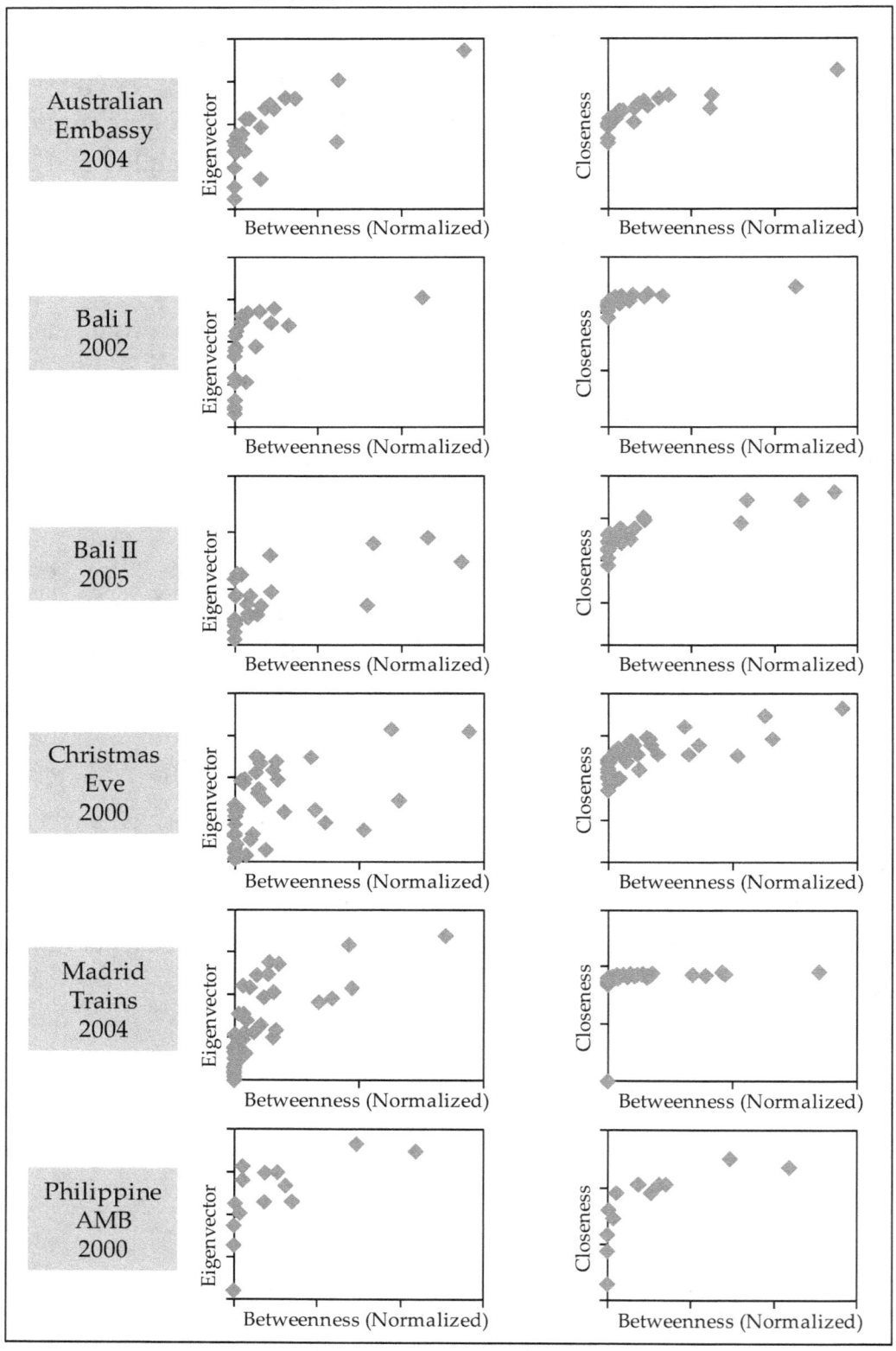

52

Some interesting characteristics arise in the distribution of eigenvector and betweenness scores across the attacks as well. Generally speaking, the cells are characterized by individuals with fairly low levels of both betweenness and eigenvector centrality. In prior research, Dominick Wright and this author showed that formation of cliques or subgroups in cells was not very strong.[86] This challenges the notion that many cells structure themselves to maintain operational security, and instead suggests that relationships among cell members grow organically over time, breaking down subgroup barriers resulting in networks with greater density of social ties over time. As the barriers between cliques break down and the participants build more relationships, fewer individuals act as boundary spanners linking distinct subgroups. Having said that, there are some subgroup divides that persist, and in each attack there are one to three individuals who span the remaining partitions.

The other common element is that the groups generally show a tendency toward lower eigenvector scores, meaning that there are relatively few individuals who connect to well-connected nodes. The best possible explanation for this pattern across cells lies in the even distributions of edges or ties across members. Again, Dominick Wright and this author argued that targeted removal in terrorist cells might have little structural effect, because there were very few hubs in the networks.[87] This violated a common feature of networks whereby a small number of nodes maintain the majority of connections. The typical manifestation is that 20 percent of the individuals maintain 80 percent of the relationships, but the study of hubs in attack cells showed that they not only failed to reach an 80-20 standard but also a missed a lower threshold whereby 20 percent of nodes had 50 percent of the connections. Instead, social ties are distributed relatively evenly across the participants. An even distribution of ties means that there is a lack of hubs or well-connected individuals, and this explains the relatively low eigenvector centrality. Since there are few hubs, there are few gatekeepers.

The Node Taxonomy in aggregate shows that terrorist cells can be operationally effective, since each of these groups conducted successful terrorist attacks, without having a significant distribution of supercharged individuals. There are relatively few gatekeepers, boundary spanners and super brokers in these networks. That might be the result of increasing social density over time whereby these groups continue to share

---

[86] Helfstein and Wright (2011).
[87] Ibid.

ideas, break down group barriers and foster an egalitarian community. This also confirms prior insights that specific individuals rarely play a structurally important role in these networks. Specific individuals like logisticians or bomb makers may turn out to be operationally critical, but the isolated removal of such members does not really affect the social structure of these well-integrated groups.

The patterns observed in the Pathway Taxonomy differ markedly from those in the Node Taxonomy. While the number of supercharged nodes in these groups may be limited, pathways through the network seem to play a critical function. Cell members display reasonably high closeness scores across the attacks. This means that there are many short paths that participants can use to access one another. People have relatively close relationships, and therefore that the transfer of radical ideas, operational instructions and material resources should flow with relative ease through the network. It is also worth recalling that people with relatively high closeness not only facilitate transactions, but are also well suited to monitor flow through the network. This means that cells naturally develop into fairly close networks in which monitoring is an organizational strength, which would seem particularly important in violent clandestine activities.

Figure 8 summarizes the characteristics across the two taxonomies for comparison. Both have very few individuals who serve simply as brokers, with modestly higher counts of those who serve either as super brokers or market makers. There is a stark contrast, however, when one looks at the central tendencies in the left-hand quadrants. There are a number of facilitators and comparatively fewer gatekeepers. It would seem that the structural strengths of these networks largely derive from the edges, or social ties that create pathways through the network, rather than the prominent position of nodes. These networks are ideally structured to facilitate communication, monitor activity and transfer ideas.

The taxonomies offer a method to summarize many different data points and extract a clearer picture of the social networks that perpetrate violent activity. The importance of social relationships is evident in both the lone wolf data and cell structure taxonomies. The next section examines the nature of these social relationships on individual radicalization and participation.

Figure 8: Distribution of Network Roles

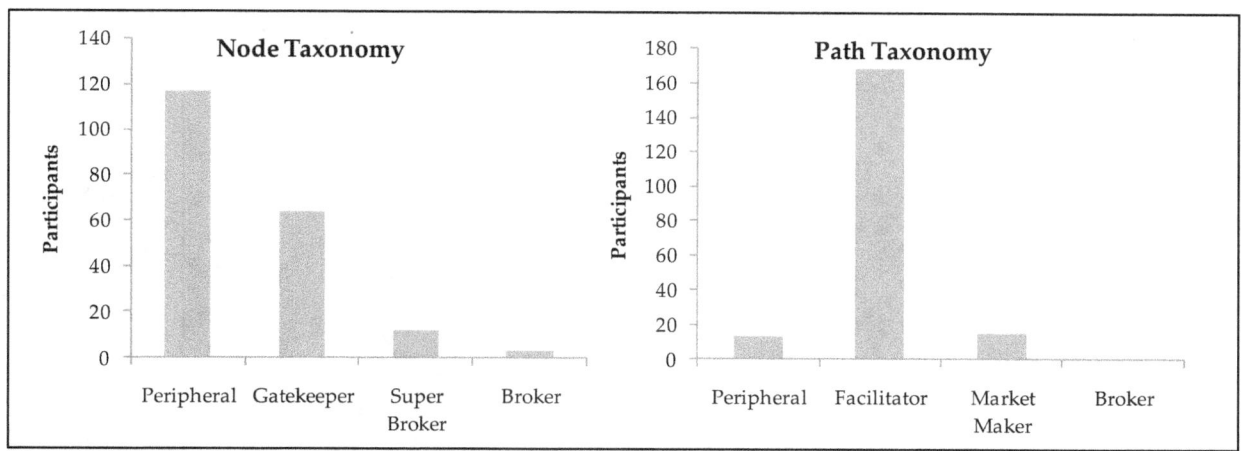

It is also interesting to examine how individual roles change within the social structure over time. The taxonomies offer a method for exploring those relationships by adding a time component to the scatterplot diagram. Figure 9 shows the Node Taxonomy for the individuals with normalized time scale across the attacks. Those closest to the origin of the plot spent the least amount of time in the cells, and are best characterized as the newest recruits. There are some interesting patterns that emerge when incorporating the time spent connected to the giant component, which in this case is the mobilized group. The graphics in Figure 7 reflect a modest increasing correlation between eigenvector and betweenness scores, which is also reflected by Figure 9, but this increasing relationship is not constant over time. For those with low levels of betweenness, eigenvector centrality increases the longer someone is part of the group. This is hardly surprising since people should form more relationships, some of which will be with well-connected individuals, the longer the involvement interval.

Figure 9: Node and Path Taxonomies over Time

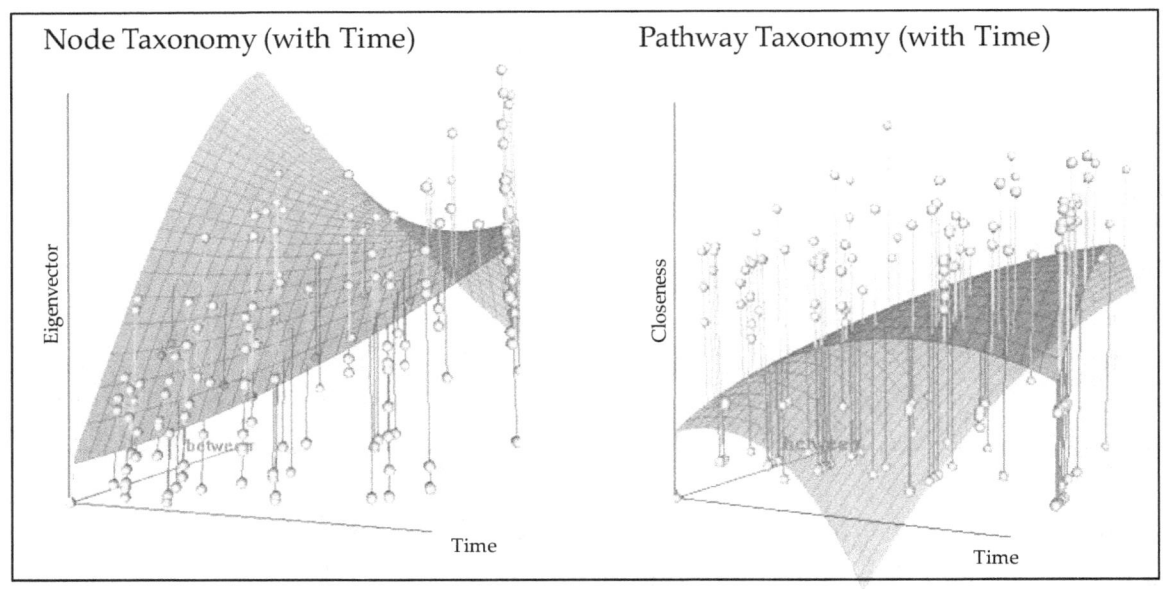

At high levels of betweenness this relationship flips completely, creating a saddle point. Those who score high in boundary spanning actually have lower eigenvector scores given longer periods of connectivity. Boundary spanners who are relatively new to groups connect with well-connected individuals, but those involved for some time actually have far fewer such connections. This may be a product of group evolution whereby those deeply involved early on become increasingly surrounded by their trusted cadre with relatively less access to new recruits. These "old hands" may be a critical bridge between early subgroups that persist, but they may fail to make many new connections as entrants arrive. By contrast, newer participants—those that join closest to attack—may have high betweenness for one of two reasons. First, they may serve a function such as weapons acquisition or logistical coordination that brings them in contact with people from many different cliques. It is reasonable to believe that people of functional importance would also connect with well-connected individuals. The second possibility is that these new entrants bring reasonably large subgroups or cliques with them. In such cases, new recruits have high betweenness because they serve as the conduit into their subgroup.

Generally speaking, as people remain involved for longer periods of time, the positive relationship correlation between eigenvector and betweenness scores actually disappears. At the middle time points, the positive correlation gives way to a flattened relationship with no correlation and then ultimately a nonlinear relationship at the extreme end of the duration scale. This nonlinear correlation, for those with the longest periods of involvement, is again marked by increases and then decreases. For the early adopters, those serving as boundary spanners are less likely to be gatekeepers. This means that there is a systemic relationship between people's position in the taxonomy and their period of involvement, but it functions in some unexpected ways.

The prior assessment of the Pathway Taxonomy, betweenness and closeness, reflected a positive relationship between closeness and betweenness. Individuals with a higher betweenness score often had higher closeness centrality. It also showed that groups tended to have reasonably high closeness scores, which was not surprising given the facilitation and monitoring benefits. Incorporating the time spent as part of the giant component into the taxonomy reveals that veteran members tend to have higher closeness, but there is some nonlinearity. Those who have been in the cell the longest score modestly lower in both betweenness and closeness. This means that individuals grow increasingly embedded in the network with longer involvement, which is not surprising, but again reflects a systemic tendency toward sustainment of the social status quo over time.

Radicalization studies often emphasize profiles or pathways associated with the individuals involved but place less emphasis on people who act as the social gateways to involvement. If social relationships are crucial to radicalization, as this project argues, people who act as gateways are particularly important in this process. Over time, individuals will grow increasingly embedded in the social network by meeting new people, but they must be brought into the group before that occurs. Terrorism studies have long recognized the importance of recruiters and recruitment, extremism's sales personnel who contribute to group sustainability by getting individuals to join the cause.[88] Despite the recognition that such individuals may play a critical role, there is limited knowledge about their patterns of behavior. Further, it is unclear if recruitment is a specialized function carried out by specific individuals or whether it is distributed across the network with all participants at one time or another serving this function. It is important to explore these gateways to social involvement.

The social journey of embedding in a radical group must begin somewhere. The first initiation into group, or the first social contact with a member already involved with the giant component, is referred to here as the gateway. This first relationship sets the stage for subsequent introductions and tie development, thereby acting as the gateway for social interconnectivity and ideological validation. It is not clear who serves as the gateway. The recruiter model would suggest that there are specific people tasked with attracting new individuals, but it is also reasonable to predict that every group member acts as a gateway at one time or another given the decentralized nature of cell formation. This begs the question whether there are specific people one can target to limit the flow of new members into the cell by eliminating a single gateway, or whether the flow is distributed evenly across members.

The histogram on the left side of Figure 10 shows the distribution of participants based on the number of times a given individual acted as a gateway. The empirics suggest that the truth lies somewhere in between these two ideals. The vast majority of participants will never actually serve as a gateway, which offers reason to doubt the "every person is a recruiter" model. This finding, though, is tempered by the fact that

---

[88] Leiken reflects the traditional notion of recruitment in Robert S. Leiken, "Europe's Angry Muslims," *Foreign Affairs* 84, no. 4 (July/August 2005), pp. 120-135.

the vast majority of new participants are brought into the giant component by people who will ultimately recruit one, two or three individuals, reflected by the graph on the right side of Figure 10. This gives reason to question the typical recruitment model, but there are a few outliers that do recruit a large number of people (six to eight) who seem to operate in a manner consistent with the recruitment model. The conclusion that one should draw from this simple assessment is that neither explanation adequately explains the empirical findings. There exist some people who serve as a gateway for a larger number of individuals, perhaps because they are tasked to do so or simply as result of being skilled social and psychological operators. The majority of people who ultimately became involved in these cells did not come through these stereotypical recruitment gateways, but became involved through less structured means.

Figure 10: Recruits by Recruiter History

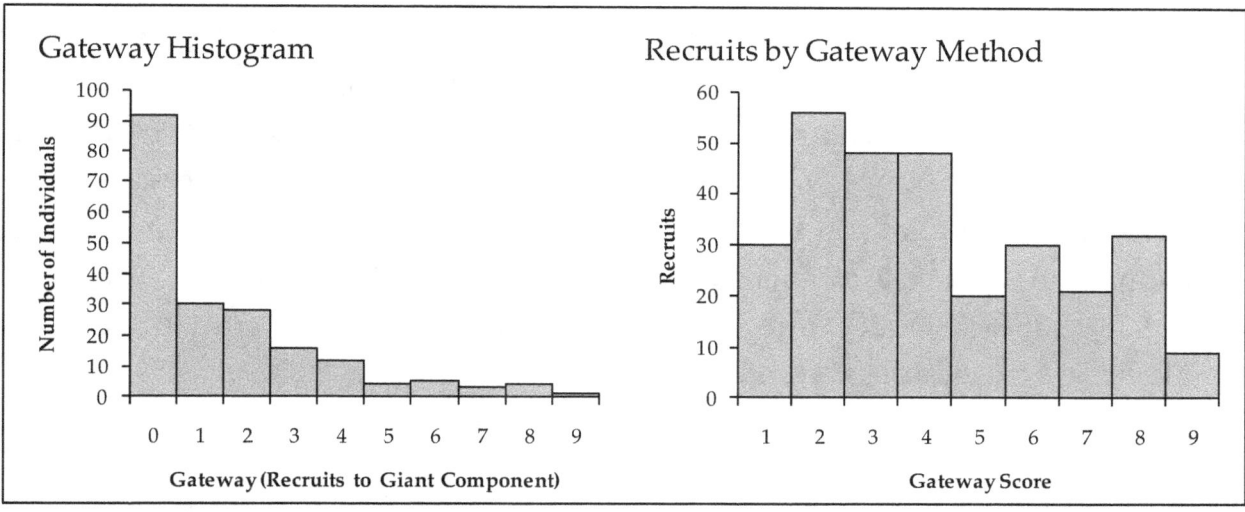

Given the distribution of recruitment within the networks, it is logical to see whether there is any specific social profile associated with those who tend to serve as gateways. The taxonomies, again, can be helpful in addressing this question by exhibiting the social characteristics of people that are most likely to bring in new individuals. The additional gateway axis is treated in a familiar fashion whereby the original vertical and horizontal axes are complimented by the number of times that individuals served as a gateway into the primary group. The modified Node Taxonomy in Figure 11 reveals some nonlinearity that is consistent with prior patterns in the study. As individuals are more connected to well-connected individuals, represented by increases in eigenvector score, there is greater tendency to bring new recruits into the network. The impact of betweenness, the tendency to link distinct cliques, is not so straightforward. Those with high and low betweenness scores—participants either nestled within a small subgroup or those spanning boundaries—do not tend to recruit a vast number of individuals. Individuals with moderate levels of betweenness are the most likely culprits. This suggests that gatekeepers are more likely to recruit individuals than boundary spanners are, but super brokers represent an exception to the rule by serving as a common gateway. Since these individuals are well connected across communities, this is not surprising, but it is interesting that ordinary boundary spanners do not play such a role.

The Path Taxonomy, with betweenness on the horizontal axis and closeness on the vertical axis, is also found in Figure 11. The relationship between betweenness and first contact remains nonlinear and concave down, meaning that recruitment first increases and then decreases as betweenness increases. The correlation of closeness and first contacts shows an increasing pattern that is concave up. This means that people with modest closeness scores tend toward less recruitment than those with lower or higher scores, but the general trend shows that those with higher closeness are much more likely to serve as gateways. Those people characterized as social facilitators, therefore, seem to play a critical role in bringing new people into the network. Given that these individuals are also well positioned to monitor the behavior of others and assist in transfer or transactions between members, they appear to play a crucial role in the development of radical cells.

The social or network characteristics have proved to have systemic relationship with patterns of radicalization, but it is also interesting to consider the impact of personal attributes to assess whether there are systemic characteristics among those more likely to serve as gateways. Statistical analysis shows that there are systemic personal factors that tie to recruitment.[89] Mirroring the results from the Social-Affinity hypothesis, there is a nonlinear relationship between gateways and schooling. Those with secular and radical schooling were more likely to draw new members into the group than those

---

[89] The results presented are for a negative binomial regression, since recruits are a count variable and there is overdispersion. Results are robust to linear specification as well as random effects. The regression results are presented as Variable Coefficient (Standard Errors, p-Value): School −0.71 (0.34, p<0.05), School² 0.21 (0.11, p<0.05), DoB 0.00 (0.00, p=0.26), Age Join 0.02 (0.00, p<0.10), Marriage 0.05 (0.22, p=0.83), Children 0.18 (0.08, p<0.05), Educational Achievement 0.00 (0.05, p=0.85), Formal Training 0.49 (0.21, p<0.05), Constant −0.36 (0.73, p=0.62).

with religious or Islamic schooling were. Age at the time of the attack did not correlate with recruitment, but there was a positive relationship between the age when people joined and recruitment. That is to say, people who joined the jihad later in life were more likely to bring others into the cell. There are many explanations for this behavior. One might be that these people simply have more and stronger social ties that they can leverage by virtue of longer life and more experience. An alternative explanation might be that these people are more comfortable or social, and thereby better primed to influence. Choices in one's personal affairs also seem to matter. Married individuals were no more or less likely to introduce others to the giant component, but the number of children was positively correlated to recruitment. Finally, those with formal training were much more likely to serve as gateways than those without, again highlighting the possible importance of social forces or experiences in radicalization.

Figure 11: Node and Path Taxonomies with Recruitment

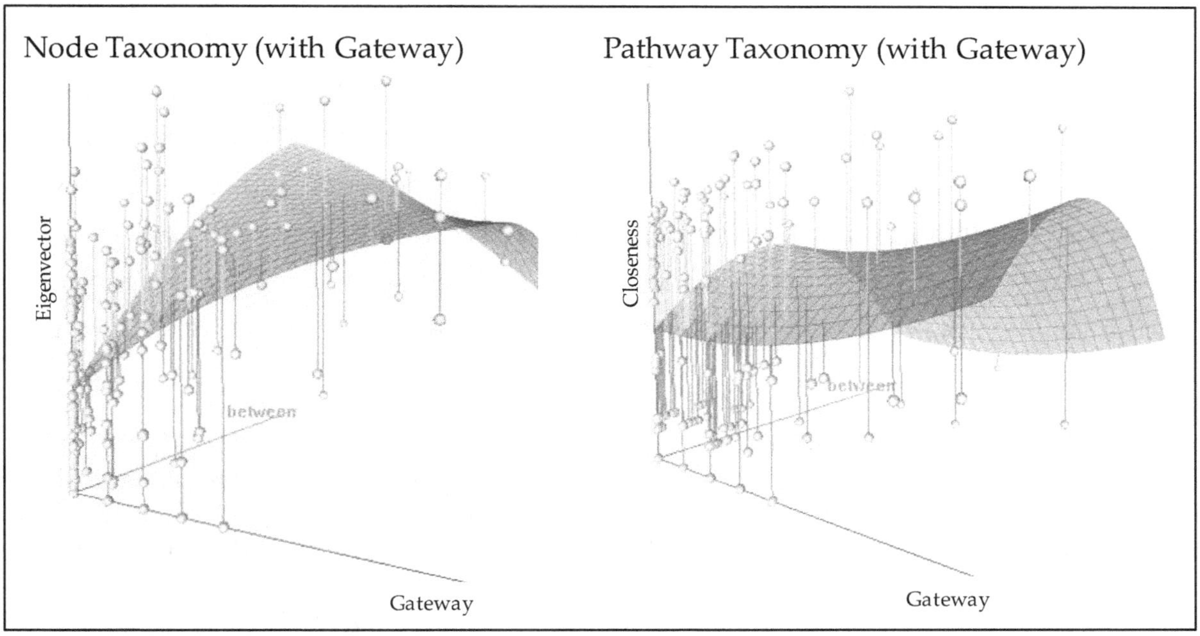

It is also possible to leverage network data for a dyadic analysis, which is to say the relationship between recruit and gateway. For example, it is possible to examine if there is there a tendency for people to recruit those with similar characteristics as a homophily theory might predict.[90] Across the personal attributes, there is evidence of

[90] Miller McPherson, Lynn Smith-Lovin and James M. Cook, "Birds of a Feather: Homophily in Social Networks," *Annual Review of Sociology* 27 (2001), 415–444.

homophily in education, but no evidence across formal training and occupation levels.[91] Those with higher educational achievement were more likely to draw others with higher education levels.[92] This is tempered by the fact that the higher one's education level, the more likely that there is a gap between the recruiter and recruit where the former is more educated.[93] Together this means that there is tendency for well-educated people to recruit other well-educated individuals, but the symmetry in education level decreases as the recruiter education level gets relatively high. Very highly educated people, it would seem, have a difficult time bringing in equally well-educated people, while still having a higher likelihood of making connections with educated individuals. The absence of homophily in formal training and occupation also needs to be tempered by a caveat: the gateway did not have a dyadic correlation with the new entrant, but the cells with more trained individuals and more professional workers were more likely to attract individuals with similar backgrounds.[94]

Combing findings in network structures with the modest tendency toward homophily, it is reasonable to ask whether recruitment activities affect social position as the cell evolves. Those who recruit more individuals are building ties for themselves as they do so, but the gateway concept also highlights the fact that new entrants subsequently build relationships with many other individuals in the network. On the one hand, it would seem intuitive that building ties through recruitment would change social position. On the other hand, the gradual building of ties within cells over time might make this irrelevant. It is also important to realize that increasing ties, or degree

---

[91] Occupation levels distinguish between unskilled, skilled and professional.

[92] Analysis relied on linear regression model with recruit education level as the dependent variable. The regression results are presented as Variable Coefficient (Standard Errors, p-Value): Gateway Education Level 0.21 (0.07, p<0.01), Average Cell Education Level 0.84 (0.19, p<0.01), Gateway Closeness −0.02 (0.00, p<0.01), Constant 0.37 (0.32, p=0.26).

[93] Analysis relied on linear regression model with the difference between the gateway and recruit education level as the dependent variable. The regression results are presented as Variable Coefficient (Standard Errors, p-Value): Gateway Education Level 0.78 (0.07, p<0.01), Average Cell Education Level 0.84 (0.19, p<0.01), Gateway Closeness −0.02 (0.00, p<0.01), Constant 0.37 (0.32, p=0.26).

[94] The first analysis relied on linear regression model with recruit formal training as the dependent variable. The regression results are presented as Variable Coefficient (Standard Errors, p-Value): Gateway Training 0.04 (0.06, p=0.51), Average Cell Training 0.60 (0.22, p<0.01), Gateway Closeness 0.00 (0.00, p<0.10), Constant 0.07 (0.05, p=0.21). The second analysis relied on linear regression model with recruit occupation type as the dependent variable. The regression results are presented as Variable Coefficient (Standard Errors, p-Value): Gateway Occupation Level −0.03 (0.06, p=0.64), Average Cell Occupation Level 1.33 (0.16, p<0.01), Gateway Closeness 0.00 (0.00, p=0.12), Constant −0.08 (0.18, p=0.65).

centrality score, might not have much impact on other measures of centrality like betweenness or closeness.

An empirical analysis that was designed to address this issue looked at individuals' network position, based on the different centrality scores used throughout. It compared scores when individuals first joined the giant component relative to those when the attack was finally conducted. Since people must be part of the larger cell before they can serve as gateways, any recruitment happens subsequent to the initial connection. The statistical analyses reflect a strong relationship between recruitment and most measures of centrality. The more times someone acted as a gateway, the greater the increase in degree, betweenness and closeness. Bringing new entrants to the group led to an increase in connection, an increase in brokerage capability between subgroups and an increase in facilitation or monitoring abilities. The only measure that did not show a significant statistical correlation was the change in eigenvector score, meaning that individuals become more connected themselves, but not necessarily to well-connected nodes. Acting as gateway, therefore, is an effective method for altering the social structure of the network and one's position within it.

This highlights an interesting and under recognized issue pertaining to the utility of recruitment. The typical recruitment model or explanation casts gatekeepers as being ideologically driven, operating with the goal of spreading the radical doctrine to new individuals. The social network analysis casts this behavior in a different light. Recruitment, or serving as a gateway to entry, is actually a method by which individuals can improve their social standing within a group, possibly gaining more control over group activities, improving agenda setting capacity or playing a more important role in managing resource flow. Development of new radical individuals may offer peripheral individuals, or even those with fairly strong position, an opportunity to improve their standing. In this sense, recruitment may not be the purview of committed ideologues but rather self-serving individuals looking to improve their social standing or power base within the cell. It is also possible, given the distribution of recruitment, that some individuals might be seeking validation of their own beliefs rather than simply pushing the doctrine to others. This offers a different perspective on recruitment, driven somewhat less by ideological fervor and instead increasing emphasis on the individual benefits or utility derived from engaging in that activity.

CONCLUSIONS AND IMPLICATIONS

This project aimed at addressing the complex and difficult problem of radicalization through the study of social processes. Studies of high-risk activism recognize the importance of social relationships, but this is often overlooked in studies of terrorist radicalization.

This report used a four-stage model of radicalization that a prototypical individual might travel along as he or she moves toward political violence. It is important to characterize these different stages, because the importance of social influence changes as people progress. Social relationships become increasingly important with the progression from awareness to interest, and peak in the acceptance stage. The tendency to form new relationships in the group then declines, despite the fact that the group actually continues adding new members up until the time of attack. Developing new relationships becomes less important once individuals come to adopt the radical beliefs, provided there are sufficient social ties to sustain involvement.

Analysis also shows that there is a nonlinear relationship between social ties and ideological affinity, whereby those primed for affinity through radical schooling have as many close social ties as those with completely secular schooling do. Individuals in between these two extremes average fewer close connections, challenging conventional wisdom about ideological predisposition and social relationships. Even those with the biographical or personaonalogical characteristics that might seem to increase the likelihood of radical behavior still find social relationships critical.

The analysis of domestic terrorism data shows that, to date, there is little evidence of lone wolf jihadists. There are very few people who progress to violent action in isolation, and those that do are often motivated by other forces such as mental health issues or other political grievances. Many radicals have a history of social contact, or they get caught in the process of developing relationships.

By contrast, the role of self-serving extremism has not been well recognized. Individuals who recruit others gain social status for their efforts, meaning that the spread of extremism may be just as much a function of self-interest as ideological fervor. The first contact, or the gateway, into an extremist cell is most likely someone who recruits one, two or three other participants, as opposed to the few recruiters who attract large numbers of people. This means that growth of radical groups is a self-organizing process driven by aggregation of individual behavior. The self-organization produces cells that have many people with high closeness centrality, or easy access to others, meaning that the groups are well suited to facilitation and monitoring. By contrast, cells are much less likely to have many gatekeepers or brokers.

There are a number of practical conclusions and implications spanning the policy and tactical realms resulting from the research. Each of these is explored below, but the common theme is that integrating the social process into models of radicalization provides greater conceptual specificity for the countering violent extremism agenda and offers some counterintuitive insights with relevant policy implications.

Conceptual Precision in Countering Radical Ideology

Many acknowledge that countering violent ideologies and winning the information war is a critical element in counterterrorism. Despite that recognition, countering ideology is probably perceived or defined differently across the spectrum of pertinent actors. The phrase "countering violent extremism" conjures up notions that one might be able to eliminate such a threat by falsifying the underlying idea or finding the loophole that invalidates its ideology. Unfortunately, ideology and belief systems do not act in a way conducive to such an approach. It is important to study the radical ideologies that present a threat, but doing so in the hopes of invalidating them will not prove effective. Ideas, despite their validity or truth, can and do motivate action. Invalidating them, therefore, is not merely an act of finding a conflicting argument to the mobilizing doctrine but rather a process much like radicalization itself.

Understanding the radical doctrine is an important element in countering the ideas, but it is a first step and a fairly small one at that. The most important aspect is understanding how and why ideologies resonate and ultimately mobilize individuals from a social, behavioral and even biological perspective. Understanding how and why certain arguments permeate belief systems and norms is critical to preventing the spread of violent extremism. Thus, more important than the ideas themselves is the way that humans rewire themselves, either socially or neurologically, to accept the ideas being advanced. The argument here is that social process is not simply important but is inseparably intertwined with radicalization. This is a valuable insight, but it is merely a first step to understanding how radical ideas come to resonate within individuals and guide their behavior.

Today, one might argue that the West invalidated communism, an ideology that has been at the heart of much political violence, but the process took the better part of century, and it remains a mobilizing force nonetheless. Acknowledging that countering violent extremism is not simply a matter of encapsulating and falsifying its ideology but actually understanding its resonance socially, behaviorally and biologically is an important beginning. Invalidating the ideology, however, will require a process whereby the ineffective and corrupt nature of its ideas must be displayed repeatedly over time.

Defusing Radicalization and the Role of Social Stages

The analysis here offers some important insights for disrupting the radicalization process, some of which are counterintuitive. It might seem that disrupting radicalization early is the easiest route to preventing people from pursuing violent ends, but there are reasons to doubt such an assessment. The barriers to entry in the early stages of awareness and interest are rather low. If the trajectory of social relationships is an indicator, the barriers increase through the acceptance stage and then decline. Since the barriers to entry are relatively low, there is little need for commitment, meaning that people are more subject to whim. Stopping someone from investigating ideas is a difficult endeavor at best. The best place to disrupt radicalization is the area where the costs are greatest, the acceptance stage, and therefore the most difficult to overcome. Intervening at this point, although running the risk of waiting too long, is likely to prove the most effective in defusing radicalization.

It is important to note that the idea of disrupting individual radicalization early is different from consistently displaying the ineffective and corrupt nature of the ideology. That is the best strategy to prevent people from ultimately paying attention, let alone succumbing to logical or emotional appeals. Relying on such a grand strategy to disrupt individual radicalization in the short run, however, may not prove the best approach to ensuring security. Instead, platforms must be developed that are capable of identifying people already working through the awareness and interest stages, then geared to exploit the barriers to entry and the importance of social relationships in the acceptance stage to intervene and redirect such individuals. This type of micro-level assessment and action is not a traditional area of strength for large bureaucratic institutions, but it will prove the critical element in promoting security over the short term as the broader ideological conflict plays out.

Extremist Websites and the Facebook-ization of the Internet

The historical record shows that lone wolf attacks are both very deadly and pose a serious threat, but lone wolf jihadist activity has not really manifested itself in any widespread fashion. There is a persistent and perhaps not unwarranted fear that teenagers will emerge from their basements after hours of exposure to online radical material and be full-blown terrorists. This remains in the realm of possibility, but the likelihood of observing this behavior on any expansive scale is small. The bigger threat is that these people find their social ties and validation through online social media. If radicalization is an interactive process as argued here, then the opportunity for interaction is critical. Traditional push avenues of radicalization like YouTube and extremist websites play a valuable role in building awareness and interest, and may also prove important in offering tactical guidance during the implementation stage, but acceptance requires other catalysts.

The nature of social interaction, especially among young people, is changing. A well-worded Twitter message, according to work by Paul Zak, can facilitate the release of as much oxytocin as someone's loved one walking into a room. It is increasingly common to see Facebook friends who have never met before embrace one another like long-lost friends. This means that online interaction through social media and other outlets can provide the critical catalyst needed for validation and norm adoption as people progress through the stages of radicalization. Social media can make extremist propaganda interactive in very dangerous ways. Each aspect of this issue represents a newly emerging trend, and as such we do know much about the process. It is clear that technology and social media are changing the way a generation interacts, but it is unclear how those changes will manifest and what the effects will ultimately be. It is also evident that violent radicals will try to exploit these technologies; but again, it is unclear how they will choose to do so. Together, this makes it very difficult to predict how people will respond to online extremist social media and networking. The first line of defense is encouraging parent and community monitoring of this activity. One benefit is that many of these forums are open to the public, and those that are not should be recognized as unique threats. There may also be the need to monitor and track activities in these realms with increasing diligence to ensure that they do not inject the crucial aspect of social validation at the right stage of the radicalization process.

Counterculture and Jihad

There appears little evidence in support of lone wolf jihadism to date, but it is neither impossible nor improbable. The instances that come closest represent a different troubling trend, which is best described as the conjoining of jihad and counterculture activity. Many of the Americans who turn toward jihad to express their political grievance have a history of counterculture activity prior to violent activity. Repeated traffic violations are common, but many escalate to other activities such as weapons possession. Those who avoid trouble with law may cycle through different religions, often breaking from them because of doctrinal disagreements. On one level, this is typical seeking behavior, but repeated disagreements over doctrine also represent typical counterculture activity. This presents a difficult set of issues for policymakers and practitioners.

As people predisposed to counterculture activity funnel their grievances and activity into jihad, it begs the question whether counterculture jihad should be treated as al-Qa'ida's global jihad or something else. Is it terrorism or typical counterculture behavior? On the one hand, the minimal adherence to jihad and predisposition to counterculture activity suggest that it be viewed as distinct phenomenon. On the other hand, treating this threat as something other than terrorism runs the risk of minimizing one of al-Qa'ida's best pathways toward more mainstream violent mobilization. A corresponding emerging trend is the concept of "jihadi cool," making extremism not simply a devout life choice but a socially redeeming and adventurous pathway. This dovetails with the increasingly counterculture nature of Western jihad in troubling ways, making it all the more important for policymakers to consider these difficult issues.

Radicalization Pathways and Threat Assessment

There are also tactical implications that emerge from this research, since different radicalization routes are likely to generate different threats. For example, those who skip stages are likely to radicalize fast and also spend less time planning. These individuals pose a unique challenge because the window for intervention is short, since the bridge from radicalization to mobilization is rapid. As a result of this shortened process, there is likely to be less planning, meaning attacks are less likely to use highly technical means. It is possible that someone along this trajectory builds or acquires a sophisticated weapon, but it more likely to be lower level technology such as firearms. By contrast, those individuals who progress along the prototypical radicalization process offer more time for interdiction but may utilize planning time to develop a more sophisticated attack. Further, a longer process probably means that individuals will develop more extensive social ties that can be leveraged for resources or knowledge.

Those who skip stages, therefore, are likely to offer few signs of their impending activity and display quick activation patterns and will often pursue simple attack plans. People that move through all of the stages will offer more signals, but will probably engage in more careful planning with more lethal technologies. It is also important to note the role of feedback loops in radicalization, particularly because they can foster a false sense of security. People may be prone to backsliding at almost any stage. Before accepting a new ideology, people may slide back to the awareness stage, and might even backslide after actually conducting an attack. The positive element of backsliding is that people move further from violence, but that process can also be deceiving. By virtue of moving away from violence, resource constrained counterterrorism and deradicalization efforts may perceive a diminished threat despite the fact that the individuals remain squarely in the midst of radicalization.

Socially Self-Serving Extremism

In an attempt to understand sources of violent extremism, placing an emphasis on its underlying ideological doctrine may have masked a simple factor driving the spread: good old-fashioned social standing and self-interest. Individuals who recruit others, or serve as the gateway, tend to have better social standing in the group over time. It is possible that the counterterrorism experts and the scientists that support their efforts have overemphasized the role that ideology plays in spreading radical doctrine. Understanding the doctrine is critical to understanding the movement, but it may play less of role in explaining why the movement spreads and changes as it does. There are, however, social benefits involved for those who actively spread a group's radical ideas and find new adherents. These people are likely to have more power in their social network, and may well accrue ego benefits from convincing others to participate. Recruitment might actually serve to validate or enhance one's beliefs, since most teachers will admit that they know a subject better after having to educate others. That would mean that macro explanations of spread may be traced to micro level activities of ego-driven individuals. This represents a different way of thinking about the macro phenomena of spread and recruitment.

The social and ideological aspects become inexorably intertwined through the radicalization and recruitment process, meaning that efforts to address them must consider both in tandem. This is difficult since both ideology and social behavior are difficult and complex on their own, but it is critical in dealing with the problem of violent extremism.

Next Steps in Decoding Radicalization

This project was intended to move the radicalization discussion and debates a few more yards down a long field. There is a great deal to be done, and two areas will prove tremendously important in the development of efficient and effective policies. First, almost all studies of radicalization to date have no variance in the independent variable: radicalization. That is to say, a great deal of information exists on those who have actually pursued a radical path, but little if anything is known about those who have rejected it. As a byproduct, most studies of radicalization are limited to explaining patterns of radicalization among a sample where everyone was a radical. This is a serious limitation in the research method and resulting insights. Rather than focus exclusively on the individuals involved in violence, building broader social networks of friends who may have had an opportunity to join but did do so would prove tremendously useful. Another approach might involve pair wise experiments between friends where one radicalized and another did not. Both of these efforts, along with other approaches to understand radicalization, would require intensive data collection efforts.

Another central question that perplexes students of the radicalization phenomenon is how it actually happens. If efforts are made to understand receptivity to violent ideology, rather than just the ideology itself, the process by which radicalization occurs assumes great importance. What is the biological, specifically neurobiological, process that occurs as people come to adopt new radical views? Does radicalization reduce individual use of traditional rational choice cost-benefit trade-off in favor of an emotional response, or does the nature of the cost-benefit trade-off itself change? Do people use different parts of the brain in responding to stimulus as they radicalize, or are the parts they use rewired with this new information? How does social validation facilitate these changes? These are just a few of the issues that lie at the heart of the radicalization puzzle.